Super Easy Diabetic Cookbook

Quick and Delicious Recipes for Blood Sugar Control

Valter Sven

Table of Contents

Introduction

Understanding Diabetes and Nutrition

Diabetes is a chronic condition that affects how the body processes glucose, a type of sugar that serves as the primary source of energy for our cells. In people with diabetes, the body either doesn't produce enough insulin (the hormone responsible for regulating blood sugar) or doesn't use insulin properly. This leads to elevated blood sugar levels, which can cause serious health complications if left unmanaged.

There are two main types of diabetes:

- **Type 1 diabetes** is typically diagnosed in childhood or adolescence and is characterized by the body's inability to produce insulin. People with Type 1 diabetes must take insulin to manage their condition.
- **Type 2 diabetes** is more common and often develops later in life. It occurs when the body becomes resistant to insulin or doesn't produce enough of it. Unlike Type 1, Type 2 diabetes can often be managed with lifestyle changes such as diet and exercise, though medication may be necessary in some cases.

Understanding the relationship between diabetes and nutrition is critical for maintaining healthy blood sugar levels. A well-planned diet can help prevent blood sugar spikes and dips, providing the body with the nutrients it needs while keeping glucose levels steady.

The Importance of a Balanced Diet

A balanced diet is essential for managing diabetes. It's not just about cutting out sugar; it's about creating meals that provide a steady source of energy, maintain stable blood sugar levels, and nourish the body.

A diabetic-friendly diet should include a variety of the following food groups:

- **Vegetables**: Non-starchy vegetables like spinach, broccoli, and peppers are rich in vitamins, minerals, and fiber. They help maintain stable blood sugar levels and contribute to overall health.
- **Whole Grains**: Whole grains like quinoa, brown rice, and whole wheat are high in fiber, which helps slow down the absorption of sugar into the bloodstream. Avoid refined grains, which can cause blood sugar spikes.

- **Lean Proteins**: Chicken, turkey, fish, and plant-based proteins like beans and tofu help build and repair tissues while keeping you full without spiking blood sugar.
- **Healthy Fats**: Avocados, olive oil, and nuts provide essential fatty acids that promote heart health and help keep you satiated.
- **Fruits**: While fruits contain natural sugars, choosing low-glycemic options like berries and apples can offer vital nutrients without drastically raising blood sugar levels.

By eating a balanced diet, you can manage blood sugar levels more effectively, improve insulin sensitivity, and reduce the risk of diabetes-related complications like heart disease, kidney damage, and nerve damage.

How to Enjoy Food While Managing Diabetes

One of the biggest misconceptions about a diabetic diet is that it's overly restrictive. People often think they have to give up their favorite foods entirely, but this isn't true. With thoughtful planning and substitutions, you can still enjoy delicious meals without compromising your health.

Here are some strategies to enjoy food while managing diabetes:

1. **Focus on Flavors**: Using herbs, spices, and healthy fats can elevate the taste of dishes without the need for added sugars or salt. Experiment with fresh garlic, ginger, rosemary, cumin, and more to create flavorful meals.
2. **Portion Control**: You don't need to give up your favorite foods completely, but managing portion sizes is key. A small serving of pasta or a single square of dark chocolate can still be part of your diet, as long as you balance it with other nutrient-rich foods.
3. **Mindful Eating**: Paying attention to how you eat can enhance your enjoyment of food. Take your time, chew thoroughly, and savor each bite. Mindful eating can help you recognize fullness and prevent overeating.
4. **Substitute Wisely**: Swap out ingredients that spike blood sugar for diabetic-friendly alternatives. For example, use almond flour instead of white flour, or opt for zucchini noodles instead of traditional pasta.
5. **Include Treats in Moderation**: It's possible to enjoy desserts even with diabetes. Try diabetic-friendly versions of your favorite sweets, made with sugar

substitutes like stevia or monk fruit, or opt for naturally sweetened treats like baked apples or berry parfaits.

Essential Ingredients for Diabetic-Friendly Cooking

Stocking your kitchen with the right ingredients can make it easier to prepare diabetic-friendly meals. Here are some essential ingredients to keep on hand:

- **Whole Grains**: Quinoa, barley, farro, and brown rice are excellent sources of fiber and can be used in a variety of dishes.
- **Non-Starchy Vegetables**: Vegetables like spinach, zucchini, and cauliflower are low in carbs and calories while providing a rich source of nutrients.
- **Lean Proteins**: Skinless chicken, turkey, tofu, and fish are excellent protein choices that don't raise blood sugar levels.
- **Healthy Fats**: Olive oil, avocados, and nuts are great sources of unsaturated fats that can help keep you full and maintain heart health.
- **Low-Glycemic Fruits**: Berries, apples, and pears are nutrient-dense and provide a natural sweetness without significantly raising blood sugar.

- **Legumes**: Beans, lentils, and chickpeas are high in fiber and protein, making them a filling and nutritious addition to meals.
- **Nuts and Seeds**: Almonds, chia seeds, and flaxseeds are great for adding healthy fats, fiber, and a crunchy texture to dishes.

These ingredients form the foundation of a diabetic-friendly diet and provide the flexibility to create a wide range of delicious and healthy recipes.

Tips for Using the Cookbook

To get the most out of this cookbook, here are a few tips to keep in mind as you explore the recipes:

1. **Focus on Variety**: Rotate your meals and include different food groups in each dish to ensure you're getting a wide range of nutrients.
2. **Prep in Advance**: Preparing ingredients or entire meals ahead of time can make it easier to stay on track with your diabetes management, especially on busy days.
3. **Customize Recipes**: Feel free to adjust the recipes to suit your tastes or dietary needs. For example, swap proteins or vegetables based on what's available or what you prefer.

4. **Track Your Blood Sugar**: After trying a new recipe, keep an eye on your blood sugar levels to understand how different foods affect you.

5. **Portion Sizes Matter**: Many of the recipes in this cookbook are designed to provide balanced portions, but be mindful of portion control, especially when it comes to carbohydrates.

By following these tips, you'll not only enjoy the meals in this cookbook, but also make meaningful progress in managing your diabetes.

A Word on Portion Control and Carb Counting

When it comes to managing diabetes, portion control and carb counting are critical tools that can help you maintain stable blood sugar levels. Understanding these concepts will allow you to enjoy your meals without overloading on carbohydrates or calories.

- **Portion Control**: Eating the right portion sizes ensures that you don't overeat or consume more calories and carbs than your body needs. Using smaller plates, pre-measuring ingredients, and paying attention to serving sizes can help you manage your intake more effectively.

- **Carb Counting**: Since carbohydrates have the most significant impact on blood sugar, carb counting can be an effective way to monitor your intake. Learn to read nutrition labels, track carbs in fruits, grains, and vegetables, and set daily carbohydrate goals that align with your personal needs.

By balancing portion control with mindful carb counting, you can enjoy a variety of foods while keeping your blood sugar levels in check. This approach allows you to have more flexibility in your diet without compromising your health.

Chapter 1

Energizing Breakfasts

Cinnamon-Spiced Oatmeal with Fresh Berries

A warm and comforting oatmeal dish, spiced with cinnamon and topped with fresh berries for a touch of natural sweetness. This breakfast provides a hearty start to your day with a balance of fiber and antioxidants.

Time of Preparation: 5 minutes

Cooking Time: 10 minutes

Serving Units: 2 servings

Ingredients:

- 1 cup rolled oats
- 2 cups unsweetened almond milk
- 1 tsp cinnamon
- 1 tbsp chia seeds
- 1 tsp vanilla extract
- 1/2 cup mixed fresh berries (blueberries, strawberries, raspberries)
- 1 tsp flaxseeds (optional)
- A pinch of salt

Procedure:

1. In a medium saucepan, combine the rolled oats, almond milk, chia seeds, cinnamon, and a pinch of salt. Bring the mixture to a boil.
2. Reduce the heat and simmer for 8–10 minutes, stirring occasionally, until the oats have absorbed the liquid and reached a creamy consistency.
3. Stir in the vanilla extract and let it sit for a minute.
4. Serve the oatmeal in bowls and top with fresh berries and flaxseeds for extra fiber and texture.

Nutritional Values (Per Serving):

- Calories: 210
- Carbohydrates: 35g
- Protein: 8g
- Fat: 5g
- Fiber: 8g
- Sugar: 5g

Cooking Tips:

For a creamier oatmeal, use half water and half almond milk. You can also add a tablespoon of almond butter for extra richness.

Health Benefits:

This oatmeal is packed with fiber from oats and berries, which helps regulate blood sugar levels and supports digestive health. Cinnamon may improve insulin sensitivity, making it beneficial for those managing diabetes.

Low-Carb Veggie Scramble

A quick, low-carb vegetable scramble that's rich in protein and perfect for diabetics. Packed with colorful vegetables, this breakfast is both nutritious and satisfying.

Time of Preparation: 5 minutes
Cooking Time: 7 minutes
Serving Units: 2 servings

Ingredients:

- 4 large eggs
- 1/2 cup diced bell peppers
- 1/4 cup chopped spinach
- 1/4 cup diced tomatoes
- 2 tbsp onion, finely chopped
- 1 tbsp olive oil
- Salt and pepper to taste
- Fresh parsley for garnish (optional)

Procedure:

1. Heat the olive oil in a non-stick skillet over medium heat.
2. Add the onions and bell peppers, sautéing for about 2–3 minutes until softened.
3. Stir in the spinach and tomatoes, cooking for another 1–2 minutes.
4. Beat the eggs in a bowl, season with salt and pepper, and pour them into the skillet.
5. Stir the eggs and veggies together, cooking until the eggs are scrambled and set, about 3–4 minutes.
6. Serve hot, garnished with parsley if desired.

Nutritional Values (Per Serving):

- Calories: 220
- Carbohydrates: 5g
- Protein: 18g
- Fat: 15g
- Fiber: 2g
- Sugar: 3g

Cooking Tips:
Add other non-starchy vegetables like mushrooms, zucchini, or asparagus to enhance

the flavor and nutrient profile. You can also sprinkle some low-fat cheese on top if desired.

Health Benefits:

This veggie scramble is low in carbohydrates, making it ideal for blood sugar management. The eggs provide high-quality protein, while the vegetables supply fiber and essential vitamins.

Whole Wheat Avocado Toast

A diabetic-friendly twist on the classic avocado toast. Made with whole wheat bread, creamy avocado, and a sprinkle of heart-healthy toppings, this breakfast keeps you full and energized.

Time of Preparation: 5 minutes

Cooking Time: None

Serving Units: 2 servings

Ingredients:

- 2 slices of whole wheat bread
- 1 ripe avocado
- 1 tsp lemon juice
- A pinch of salt
- A pinch of red pepper flakes (optional)
- 1 tbsp chia seeds (optional)
- Fresh cherry tomatoes, sliced (optional)

Procedure:

1. Toast the slices of whole wheat bread until golden brown.
2. In a small bowl, mash the avocado with a fork, mixing in the lemon juice and a pinch of salt.
3. Spread the mashed avocado evenly over the toasted bread.
4. Sprinkle with chia seeds and red pepper flakes, and add sliced cherry tomatoes if desired.
5. Serve immediately.

Nutritional Values (Per Serving):

- Calories: 250
- Carbohydrates: 22g
- Protein: 5g
- Fat: 18g

- Fiber: 7g
- Sugar: 1g

Cooking Tips:

For extra flavor, drizzle a bit of balsamic glaze or add a poached egg on top for more protein. You can also swap whole wheat bread for sprouted grain bread for a higher fiber content.

Health Benefits:

Avocados are rich in heart-healthy monounsaturated fats that help improve cholesterol levels. The fiber from whole wheat bread and avocado promotes better digestion and blood sugar regulation.

Greek Yogurt Parfait with Nuts

A layered breakfast parfait that combines creamy Greek yogurt with crunchy nuts and fresh fruit, delivering a refreshing and protein-packed start to your morning.

Time of Preparation: 5 minutes

Cooking Time: None

Serving Units: 2 servings

Ingredients:

- 1 cup plain, unsweetened Greek yogurt
- 1/2 cup mixed fresh berries (blueberries, strawberries, raspberries)
- 2 tbsp walnuts or almonds, chopped
- 1 tbsp chia seeds
- 1 tsp ground flaxseeds
- 1 tsp honey (optional)

Procedure:

1. In two serving glasses, add a layer of Greek yogurt.
2. Add a layer of mixed berries on top of the yogurt.
3. Sprinkle the chopped nuts, chia seeds, and flaxseeds over the berries.
4. Repeat the layers as desired, finishing with a drizzle of honey (optional).
5. Serve immediately or refrigerate for later.

Nutritional Values (Per Serving):

- Calories: 220
- Carbohydrates: 18g
- Protein: 12g
- Fat: 10g
- Fiber: 6g

- Sugar: 10g

Cooking Tips:

Use unsweetened yogurt to keep the sugar content low. You can also switch up the nuts or add sunflower seeds for a different crunch.

Health Benefits:

Greek yogurt is an excellent source of protein and probiotics, which support gut health. The nuts provide healthy fats and fiber, contributing to satiety and heart health.

Flaxseed Pancakes with Sugar-Free Syrup

Fluffy pancakes made with flaxseed meal and whole wheat flour, served with a sugar-free syrup for a diabetic-friendly breakfast that doesn't sacrifice flavor.

Time of Preparation: 10 minutes

Cooking Time: 10 minutes

Serving Units: 4 servings

Ingredients:

- 1 cup whole wheat flour
- 1/4 cup flaxseed meal
- 1 tsp baking powder
- 1/2 tsp baking soda
- 1/4 tsp salt
- 1 cup unsweetened almond milk
- 1 large egg
- 1 tbsp melted coconut oil
- 1/2 tsp vanilla extract
- Sugar-free syrup (for serving)

Procedure:

1. In a large bowl, combine the whole wheat flour, flaxseed meal, baking powder, baking soda, and salt.
2. In a separate bowl, whisk together the almond milk, egg, coconut oil, and vanilla extract.
3. Pour the wet ingredients into the dry ingredients and stir until combined.
4. Heat a non-stick skillet or griddle over medium heat. Pour 1/4 cup of batter for each pancake.
5. Cook for 2-3 minutes on each side, or until golden brown and fully cooked through.
6. Serve with sugar-free syrup.

Nutritional Values (Per Serving):

- Calories: 180
- Carbohydrates: 20g
- Protein: 6g
- Fat: 8g
- Fiber: 5g
- Sugar: 2g

Cooking Tips:

For extra flavor, you can add a pinch of cinnamon or nutmeg to the pancake batter. To make the pancakes even lighter, fold in some whipped egg whites before cooking.

Health Benefits:

Flaxseed is high in omega-3 fatty acids and fiber, promoting heart health and digestion. Using whole wheat flour ensures a slower release of glucose into the bloodstream.

Chia Seed Pudding with Almond Milk

A creamy, nutrient-packed chia seed pudding made with almond milk and naturally sweetened with a touch of vanilla. This dish is perfect for breakfast or a light snack.

Time of Preparation: 5 minutes
Chill Time: 4 hours (or overnight)
Serving Units: 2 servings

Ingredients:

- 1/4 cup chia seeds
- 1 cup unsweetened almond milk
- 1 tsp vanilla extract
- 1 tsp maple syrup or honey (optional)
- Fresh fruit for topping (optional)
- A pinch of cinnamon (optional)

Procedure:

1. In a medium-sized bowl or jar, combine the chia seeds, almond milk, vanilla extract, and maple syrup (if using).
2. Stir well to ensure that the chia seeds are evenly distributed and not clumping together.
3. Cover and refrigerate for at least 4 hours, or overnight, until the mixture thickens to a pudding-like consistency.
4. Serve with fresh fruit and a sprinkle of cinnamon if desired.

Nutritional Values (Per Serving):

- Calories: 150
- Carbohydrates: 10g
- Protein: 4g
- Fat: 9g
- Fiber: 8g
- Sugar: 1g

Cooking Tips:
Make this pudding the night before for a quick grab-and-go breakfast. You can also add a tablespoon of cocoa powder for a chocolate version.

Health Benefits:
Chia seeds are rich in omega-3 fatty acids, fiber, and antioxidants, which support heart health, digestion, and blood sugar control. Almond milk is low in carbs, making it a great choice for diabetics.

Chapter 2

Simple and Satisfying Salads

Spinach and Quinoa Salad with Lemon Vinaigrette

This nutrient-dense spinach and quinoa salad is tossed with a refreshing lemon vinaigrette. High in protein and fiber, it's a satisfying and diabetic-friendly meal or side dish.

Time of Preparation: 10 minutes

Cooking Time: 15 minutes (for quinoa)

Serving Units: 4 servings

Ingredients:

- 1 cup cooked quinoa
- 2 cups fresh spinach leaves
- 1/4 cup red onion, thinly sliced
- 1/2 cup cherry tomatoes, halved
- 1/4 cup crumbled feta cheese
- 2 tbsp chopped walnuts
- 1 tbsp olive oil
- 1 tbsp fresh lemon juice
- 1 tsp Dijon mustard
- Salt and pepper to taste

Procedure:

1. Cook the quinoa according to package instructions and let it cool.
2. In a large bowl, combine the cooked quinoa, spinach, red onion, cherry tomatoes, and walnuts.
3. In a small bowl, whisk together the olive oil, lemon juice, Dijon mustard, salt, and pepper to create the vinaigrette.
4. Drizzle the vinaigrette over the salad and toss gently.
5. Top with crumbled feta cheese and serve.

Nutritional Values (Per Serving):

- Calories: 180
- Carbohydrates: 16g
- Protein: 6g
- Fat: 11g
- Fiber: 4g
- Sugar: 2g

Cooking Tips:

Prepare extra quinoa and store it in the fridge to use in salads or other dishes throughout the week. You can also add grilled chicken for extra protein.

Health Benefits:

Quinoa is a complete protein and a good source of fiber, making it perfect for blood sugar management. Spinach provides iron, calcium, and antioxidants, while walnuts add healthy fats to support heart health.

Grilled Chicken Caesar Salad (Diabetic-Friendly)

A lightened-up version of the classic Caesar salad, featuring grilled chicken, crisp romaine lettuce, and a flavorful, homemade Caesar dressing that's low in carbs.

Time of Preparation: 15 minutes

Cooking Time: 10 minutes (for chicken)

Serving Units: 4 servings

Ingredients:

- 2 large boneless, skinless chicken breasts
- 6 cups chopped romaine lettuce
- 1/4 cup freshly grated Parmesan cheese
- 1/4 cup whole wheat croutons (optional)
- 2 tbsp olive oil
- 1 tsp garlic powder
- Salt and pepper to taste

For Dressing:

- 1/4 cup plain Greek yogurt
- 1 tbsp Dijon mustard
- 2 tbsp fresh lemon juice
- 1 clove garlic, minced
- 1 tbsp grated Parmesan cheese
- Salt and pepper to taste

Procedure:

1. Season the chicken breasts with garlic powder, salt, and pepper. Grill over medium heat for 5–7 minutes on each side, or until fully cooked. Slice and set aside.
2. In a large bowl, toss the chopped romaine lettuce with the grilled chicken and Parmesan cheese.
3. For the dressing, whisk together the Greek yogurt, Dijon mustard, lemon juice, garlic, and Parmesan cheese in a small bowl. Season with salt and pepper.

4. Drizzle the dressing over the salad and toss to combine.

5. Top with croutons, if using, and serve.

Nutritional Values (Per Serving):

- Calories: 230
- Carbohydrates: 7g
- Protein: 28g
- Fat: 10g
- Fiber: 3g
- Sugar: 1g

Cooking Tips:

For a smokier flavor, grill the chicken on an outdoor barbecue. You can also make the dressing in advance and store it in the refrigerator for up to 3 days.

Health Benefits:

This diabetic-friendly Caesar salad provides lean protein from the grilled chicken and beneficial probiotics from the Greek yogurt dressing, while keeping carbohydrate content low.

3. Cucumber and Feta Salad with Olive Oil

A refreshing, simple salad made with crisp cucumbers, tangy feta cheese, and a drizzle of olive oil. This salad is perfect for a light lunch or a side dish.

Time of Preparation: 10 minutes

Cooking Time: None

Serving Units: 4 servings

Ingredients:

- 2 large cucumbers, peeled and thinly sliced
- 1/4 cup crumbled feta cheese
- 2 tbsp extra-virgin olive oil
- 1 tbsp fresh lemon juice
- 1 tbsp chopped fresh dill (optional)
- Salt and pepper to taste

Procedure:

1. In a large bowl, combine the sliced cucumbers and crumbled feta cheese.
2. Drizzle the olive oil and lemon juice over the cucumber mixture.
3. Add the fresh dill, if using, and season with salt and pepper.
4. Toss gently and serve chilled.

Nutritional Values (Per Serving):

- Calories: 110
- Carbohydrates: 6g
- Protein: 3g
- Fat: 9g
- Fiber: 1g
- Sugar: 2g

Cooking Tips:

Use English cucumbers for a milder flavor, and

feel free to add sliced red onions or cherry tomatoes for more color and taste.

Health Benefits:

Cucumbers are hydrating and low in calories, making them excellent for blood sugar control. Feta cheese adds calcium and healthy fats, and olive oil is rich in heart-healthy monounsaturated fats.

Kale and Apple Salad with Walnuts

A crunchy and satisfying kale salad with sweet apples and toasted walnuts, tossed in a light vinaigrette. This salad offers a balance of textures and flavors, perfect for a healthy meal.

Time of Preparation: 10 minutes

Cooking Time: 5 minutes (for walnuts)

Serving Units: 4 servings

Ingredients:

- 4 cups chopped kale (stems removed)
- 1 large apple, thinly sliced
- 1/4 cup chopped walnuts
- 1 tbsp olive oil
- 1 tbsp apple cider vinegar
- 1 tsp Dijon mustard
- Salt and pepper to taste

Procedure:

1. Toast the walnuts in a dry skillet over medium heat for 2–3 minutes until fragrant. Set aside.
2. In a small bowl, whisk together the olive oil, apple cider vinegar, and Dijon mustard to make the vinaigrette.
3. In a large bowl, massage the chopped kale with a pinch of salt for about 1 minute to soften the leaves.
4. Add the sliced apple and toasted walnuts to the kale.
5. Drizzle the vinaigrette over the salad and toss well. Serve immediately.

Nutritional Values (Per Serving):

- Calories: 160
- Carbohydrates: 12g
- Protein: 3g

- Fat: 11g
- Fiber: 4g
- Sugar: 7g

Cooking Tips:

For extra sweetness, use honeycrisp or gala apples. To make the salad more filling, add some cooked quinoa or grilled chicken.

Health Benefits:

Kale is a superfood packed with vitamins A, C, and K, while apples add fiber and natural sweetness. Walnuts provide omega-3 fatty acids, which support heart health.

Tomato, Basil, and Mozzarella Salad

Short Description

A classic Italian-inspired salad featuring juicy tomatoes, fresh basil, and creamy mozzarella, drizzled with olive oil and balsamic vinegar.

Time of Preparation: 10 minutes

Cooking Time: None

Serving Units: 4 servings

Ingredients:

- 4 large ripe tomatoes, sliced
- 1 cup fresh mozzarella cheese, sliced
- 1/4 cup fresh basil leaves
- 2 tbsp extra-virgin olive oil
- 1 tbsp balsamic vinegar
- Salt and pepper to taste

Procedure:

1. Arrange the tomato slices and mozzarella on a serving platter, alternating between them.
2. Tuck fresh basil leaves in between the tomato and mozzarella slices.
3. Drizzle olive oil and balsamic vinegar over the salad.
4. Season with salt and pepper, and serve immediately.

Nutritional Values (Per Serving):

- Calories: 180
- Carbohydrates: 5g
- Protein: 8g
- Fat: 14g
- Fiber: 2g
- Sugar: 3g

Cooking Tips:

For added flavor, reduce the balsamic vinegar by simmering it over low heat until it thickens into a syrup. Serve this salad with whole-grain bread for a more complete meal.

Health Benefits:

Tomatoes are rich in lycopene, an antioxidant that may help lower the risk of heart disease. Mozzarella provides protein and calcium, while olive oil promotes heart health with its monounsaturated fats.

Roasted Beet and Arugula Salad with Balsamic

This vibrant salad features roasted beets, peppery arugula, and a balsamic vinaigrette for a refreshing and nutrient-packed dish that's both sweet and savory.

Time of Preparation: 10 minutes
Cooking Time: 30 minutes (for beets)
Serving Units: 4 servings

Ingredients:

- 3 medium beets, roasted and sliced
- 4 cups fresh arugula
- 1/4 cup goat cheese, crumbled
- 1/4 cup walnuts, chopped and toasted
- 2 tbsp balsamic vinegar
- 2 tbsp olive oil
- Salt and pepper to taste

Procedure:

1. Preheat the oven to 400°F (200°C). Wrap the beets in foil and roast for 30 minutes or until tender. Let them cool, then slice.
2. In a large bowl, combine the arugula, roasted beets, and toasted walnuts.
3. In a small bowl, whisk together the balsamic vinegar, olive oil, salt, and pepper.
4. Drizzle the vinaigrette over the salad and toss gently.
5. Top with crumbled goat cheese and serve.

Nutritional Values (Per Serving):

- Calories: 210
- Carbohydrates: 14g
- Protein: 6g
- Fat: 16g
- Fiber: 5g
- Sugar: 7g

Cooking Tips:
Roast the beets a day in advance to save time. You can also add some quinoa to this salad to make it a more filling meal.

Chapter 3

Delicious Lunches

Zucchini Noodles with Pesto and Grilled Chicken

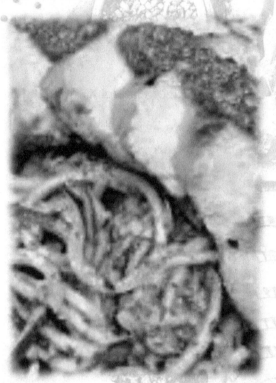

A low-carb alternative to traditional pasta, zucchini noodles are tossed with a rich pesto sauce and topped with grilled chicken, making this a perfect diabetic-friendly lunch.

Time of Preparation: 10 minutes
Cooking Time: 15 minutes
Serving Units: 2 servings

Ingredients:

- 2 medium zucchinis, spiralized into noodles
- 2 boneless, skinless chicken breasts
- 1/4 cup homemade or store-bought pesto (sugar-free)
- 1 tbsp olive oil
- 1 tbsp lemon juice
- Salt and pepper to taste
- Grated Parmesan cheese (optional)

Procedure:

1. Season the chicken breasts with salt, pepper, and lemon juice. Grill over medium heat for 5–7 minutes per side, or until fully cooked. Set aside and slice.
2. In a large pan, heat the olive oil over medium heat. Add the zucchini noodles and sauté for 2–3 minutes until just tender.
3. Remove from heat and toss the zucchini noodles with the pesto sauce.
4. Plate the zucchini noodles and top with sliced grilled chicken. Garnish with grated Parmesan if desired.

Nutritional Values (Per Serving):

- Calories: 350
- Carbohydrates: 8g
- Protein: 35g

- Fat: 20g
- Fiber: 4g
- Sugar: 3g

Cooking Tips:

You can substitute store-bought pesto with a homemade version using fresh basil, garlic, olive oil, and nuts. Be mindful of the salt content in pre-made pesto.

Health Benefits:

Zucchini noodles are a great low-carb substitute for pasta, helping to manage blood sugar levels. Chicken adds lean protein, and the healthy fats from the pesto sauce provide lasting energy.

Low-Carb Turkey and Veggie Wraps

A quick and light low-carb lunch, these turkey wraps are loaded with fresh veggies and a flavorful spread, all rolled up in a crisp lettuce leaf for a refreshing bite.

Time of Preparation: 10 minutes

Cooking Time: None

Serving Units: 2 servings

Ingredients:

- 6 large lettuce leaves (Romaine or Butter Lettuce)
- 6 slices deli turkey (low-sodium)
- 1/2 avocado, sliced
- 1/4 cup cucumber, julienned
- 1/4 cup red bell pepper, julienned
- 1 tbsp Dijon mustard or hummus
- Salt and pepper to taste

Procedure:

1. Lay out the lettuce leaves and spread a thin layer of Dijon mustard or hummus on each leaf.
2. Place a slice of turkey on top of each leaf, followed by avocado slices, cucumber, and red bell pepper.
3. Season with a pinch of salt and pepper.
4. Roll the lettuce leaf tightly around the fillings to create a wrap. Secure with a toothpick if necessary.
5. Serve immediately or wrap in foil for a portable lunch.

Nutritional Values (Per Serving):

- Calories: 180
- Carbohydrates: 6g
- Protein: 18g
- Fat: 9g
- Fiber: 4g
- Sugar: 2g

Cooking Tips:

For added flavor, you can mix some Greek yogurt with Dijon mustard for a creamy spread. If you want a bit of crunch, add some choppekd nuts or seeds inside the wraps.

Health Benefits:

These low-carb wraps are perfect for blood sugar control. The turkey provides lean protein, and the avocado offers heart-healthy fats, while the vegetables add fiber and essential nutrients.

Quinoa-Stuffed Bell Peppers

Colorful bell peppers are stuffed with a protein-packed quinoa filling, loaded with vegetables and herbs, for a wholesome, satisfying lunch that is both hearty and healthy.

Time of Preparation: 10 minutes

Cooking Time: 30 minutes

Serving Units: 4 servings

Ingredients:

- 4 large bell peppers (red, yellow, or green)
- 1 cup cooked quinoa
- 1/2 cup black beans, rinsed and drained
- 1/4 cup corn kernels (fresh or frozen)
- 1/4 cup diced tomatoes
- 1/4 cup chopped fresh cilantro
- 1 tbsp olive oil
- 1 tsp ground cumin
- 1/2 tsp smoked paprika
- Salt and pepper to taste
- 1/4 cup shredded low-fat cheese (optional)

Procedure:

1. Preheat the oven to 375°F (190°C). Cut off the tops of the bell peppers and remove the seeds and membranes.
2. In a large bowl, combine the cooked quinoa, black beans, corn, diced tomatoes, cilantro, olive oil, cumin, smoked paprika, salt, and pepper.
3. Stuff the bell peppers with the quinoa mixture and place them in a baking dish.
4. Cover with foil and bake for 25 minutes. Remove the foil and sprinkle with cheese if using, then bake for an additional 5 minutes until the cheese is melted.

5. Serve warm.

Nutritional Values (Per Serving):

- Calories: 220
- Carbohydrates: 32g
- Protein: 8g
- Fat: 7g
- Fiber: 8g
- Sugar: 6g

Cooking Tips:

You can prepare the quinoa filling in advance and store it in the fridge for up to two days. Feel free to add ground turkey or lean beef for extra protein.

Health Benefits:

Quinoa is a complete protein, providing all nine essential amino acids, while the bell peppers are rich in vitamins A and C. This meal is fiber-rich, promoting better digestion and blood sugar control.

Lentil Soup with Fresh Herbs

A hearty and nutritious lentil soup infused with fresh herbs, offering a delicious and warming meal that is rich in fiber and perfect for managing blood sugar levels.

Time of Preparation: 10 minutes

Cooking Time: 30 minutes

Serving Units: 4 servings

Ingredients:

- 1 cup dried lentils (green or brown), rinsed
- 1 medium onion, diced
- 2 cloves garlic, minced
- 2 carrots, diced
- 1 celery stalk, diced
- 6 cups low-sodium vegetable broth
- 1 tsp ground cumin
- 1/2 tsp turmeric
- 2 tbsp fresh parsley, chopped
- 1 tbsp fresh dill, chopped
- 1 tbsp olive oil
- Salt and pepper to taste

Procedure:

1. Heat the olive oil in a large pot over medium heat. Add the onion, garlic'2, carrots, and celery, and sauté for 5–7 minutes until softened.
2. Stir in the cumin and turmeric and cook for 1 minute.
3. Add the lentils and vegetable broth to the pot and bring to a boil. Reduce the heat and simmer for 25–30 minutes until the lentils are tender.
4. Stir in the fresh parsley and dill. Season with salt and pepper to taste.
5. Serve hot.

Nutritional Values (Per Serving):

- Calories: 200
- Carbohydrates: 35g
- Protein: 12g
- Fat: 4g
- Fiber: 13g
- Sugar: 4g

Cooking Tips:

For a creamier texture, use an immersion blender to partially blend the soup. Add a squeeze of lemon juice for a bright, tangy flavor before serving.

Health Benefits:

Lentils are an excellent source of plant-based protein and fiber, helping to regulate blood sugar levels. The addition of fresh herbs like parsley and dill enhances the flavor while providing antioxidants.

Grilled Salmon with Mixed Greens

A nutritious lunch featuring grilled salmon atop a bed of mixed greens, drizzled with a light lemon vinaigrette. This dish is rich in omega-3 fatty acids and essential nutrients.

Time of Preparation: 10 minutes
Cooking Time: 10 minutes
Serving Units: 2 servings

Ingredients:

- 2 salmon fillets (about 6 oz each)
- 4 cups mixed salad greens (arugula, spinach, and romaine)
- 1/2 cup cherry tomatoes, halved
- 1/4 cucumber, sliced
- 1 tbsp olive oil
- 1 tbsp lemon juice
- Salt and pepper to taste
- Lemon wedges for serving

Procedure:

1. Preheat a grill or grill pan over medium heat. Season the salmon fillets with salt and pepper.
2. Grill the salmon for 4–5 minutes per side, or until fully cooked and slightly charred.

3. In a large bowl, toss the mixed greens, cherry tomatoes, and cucumber with olive oil, lemon juice, salt, and pepper.

4. Serve the grilled salmon on top of the salad. Garnish with lemon wedges and enjoy.

Nutritional Values (Per Serving):

- Calories: 350
- Carbohydrates: 8g
- Protein: 34g
- Fat: 22g
- Fiber: 3g
- Sugar: 3g

Cooking Tips:

For extra flavor, marinate the salmon in olive oil, garlic, and lemon juice for 30 minutes before grilling. You can also add avocado slices for more healthy fats.

Health Benefits:

Salmon is an excellent source of omega-3 fatty acids, which support heart health and reduce inflammation. The mixed greens provide fiber and antioxidants, while the lemon vinaigrette adds a burst of freshness.

Chickpea Salad with Lemon Dressing

A zesty and protein-rich chickpea salad tossed with a simple lemon dressing, perfect for a light and filling lunch that's also high in fiber and essential nutrients.

Time of Preparation: 10 minutes
Cooking Time: None
Serving Units: 2 servings

Ingredients:

- 1 can (15 oz) chickpeas, rinsed and drained
- 1/4 cup red onion, finely chopped
- 1/4 cup cucumber, diced
- 1/4 cup cherry tomatoes, halved
- 2 tbsp fresh parsley, chopped
- 2 tbsp lemon juice
- 1 tbsp olive oil
- Salt and pepper to taste

Procedure:

1. In a large bowl, combine the chickpeas, red onion, cucumber, cherry tomatoes, and parsley.

2. In a small bowl, whisk together the lemon juice, olive oil, salt, and pepper.

3. Pour the lemon dressing over the chickpea mixture and toss well.

4. Serve immediately or refrigerate for later.

Nutritional Values (Per Serving):

- Calories: 220
- Carbohydrates: 28g
- Protein: 8g
- Fat: 9g
- Fiber: 9g
- Sugar: 4g

Cooking Tips:

Add some crumbled feta cheese for extra flavor, or serve the salad in lettuce wraps for a portable lunch. This salad keeps well in the fridge for up to 2 days.

Health Benefits:

Chickpeas are rich in fiber and protein, which help maintain steady blood sugar levels. The lemon dressing adds a tangy, refreshing flavor, while the fresh vegetables contribute essential vitamins and minerals.

Chapter 4

Guilt-Free Snacks

Baked Kale Chips

Crispy and delicious, these baked kale chips are a perfect guilt-free snack that satisfies cravings for something crunchy without the carbs or unhealthy fats.

Time of Preparation: 5 minutes
Cooking Time: 15 minutes
Serving Units: 4 servings

Ingredients:

- 1 large bunch of kale, stems removed and leaves torn into bite-sized pieces
- 1 tbsp olive oil
- 1/4 tsp sea salt
- 1/4 tsp garlic powder (optional)

Procedure:

1. Preheat your oven to 300°F (150°C).
2. Wash and thoroughly dry the kale leaves.
3. Toss the kale with olive oil, making sure each leaf is lightly coated. Season with salt and garlic powder if using.
4. Spread the kale leaves in a single layer on a baking sheet lined with parchment paper.
5. Bake for 12–15 minutes, or until the edges are crispy but not burnt.
6. Let cool and enjoy.

Nutritional Values (Per Serving):

- Calories: 50
- Carbohydrates: 3g
- Protein: 2g
- Fat: 4g
- Fiber: 1g
- Sugar: 0g

Cooking Tips:
Make sure the kale is completely dry before baking to get a crispier texture. You can experiment with flavors like paprika, chili powder, or nutritional yeast for a cheesy flavor.

Health Benefits:

Kale is rich in antioxidants, vitamins A, C, and K, and fiber, making these chips a nutrient-dense, low-calorie snack that supports overall health and helps regulate blood sugar levels.

Almond Butter and Celery Sticks

A classic and easy snack that pairs creamy almond butter with crunchy celery sticks, offering a perfect balance of protein, healthy fats, and fiber.

Time of Preparation: 5 minutes

Cooking Time: None

Serving Units: 2 servings

Ingredients:

- 4 celery sticks
- 2 tbsp almond butter (unsweetened and natural)
- 1/2 tsp chia seeds or flaxseeds (optional for topping)

Procedure:

1. Wash the celery sticks and cut them into 3-inch pieces.
2. Spread almond butter evenly inside each celery stick.
3. Sprinkle chia seeds or flaxseeds on top for added texture and nutrition.
4. Serve immediately.

Nutritional Values (Per Serving):

- Calories: 180
- Carbohydrates: 6g
- Protein: 5g
- Fat: 16g
- Fiber: 4g
- Sugar: 2g

Cooking Tips:

Use natural, unsweetened almond butter to avoid added sugars. You can substitute with peanut butter or sunflower seed butter if preferred.

Health Benefits:

Almond butter is packed with healthy fats, protein, and fiber, which help keep you full while maintaining steady blood sugar levels. Celery provides hydration and fiber with minimal calories.

Greek Yogurt with Sliced Almonds

Creamy Greek yogurt topped with crunchy sliced almonds creates a satisfying snack high in protein, healthy fats, and probiotics for gut health.

Time of Preparation: 3 minutes

Cooking Time: None

Serving Units: 2 servings

Ingredients:

- 1 cup plain Greek yogurt (unsweetened)
- 2 tbsp sliced almonds
- 1 tsp chia seeds (optional)
- A drizzle of honey (optional)

Procedure:

1. Divide the Greek yogurt into two bowls.
2. Top each bowl with sliced almonds and chia seeds if using.
3. Drizzle with a small amount of honey for sweetness if desired. Serve immediately.

Nutritional Values (Per Serving):

- Calories: 180
- Carbohydrates: 8g
- Protein: 15g
- Fat: 8g
- Fiber: 3g
- Sugar: 5g

Cooking Tips:

For added flavor, you can mix in some vanilla extract or cinnamon. Choose full-fat Greek yogurt for a more filling snack.

Health Benefits:

Greek yogurt is rich in protein and probiotics, which promote gut health and aid in digestion. The almonds provide healthy fats and fiber, contributing to satiety and improved blood sugar control.

Roasted Chickpeas with Spices

A crunchy and flavorful snack made by roasting chickpeas with your favorite spices. These roasted chickpeas are a high-protein, fiber-rich snack that satisfies salty cravings.

Time of Preparation: 5 minutes
Cooking Time: 30 minutes
Serving Units: 4 servings

Ingredients:

- 1 can (15 oz) chickpeas, drained and rinsed
- 1 tbsp olive oil
- 1/2 tsp smoked paprika
- 1/2 tsp ground cumin
- 1/4 tsp garlic powder
- Salt and pepper to taste

Procedure:

1. Preheat your oven to 400°F (200°C).
2. Spread the chickpeas on a paper towel to dry.
3. In a bowl, toss the chickpeas with olive oil, smoked paprika, cumin, garlic powder, salt, and pepper.
4. Spread the chickpeas in a single layer on a baking sheet.
5. Roast for 25–30 minutes, shaking the pan halfway through, until golden and crispy.
6. Let cool and enjoy.

Nutritional Values (Per Serving):

- Calories: 120
- Carbohydrates: 18g
- Protein: 5g
- Fat: 4g
- Fiber: 5g
- Sugar: 1g

Cooking Tips:

Make sure the chickpeas are completely dry before roasting for the crispiest results. Try different seasoning blends like curry powder, chili flakes, or Italian herbs.

Health Benefits:

Chickpeas are a great source of plant-based protein and fiber, which helps keep blood sugar levels stable. The olive oil provides healthy fats, and the spices add antioxidants.

Cottage Cheese and Berries

A protein-rich, low-carb snack made with creamy cottage cheese and fresh, antioxidant-packed berries. This snack is perfect for diabetics as it offers a balance of protein, fiber, and natural sweetness.

Time of Preparation: 3 minutes
Cooking Time: None
Serving Units: 2 servings

Ingredients:

- 1 cup low-fat cottage cheese
- 1/2 cup mixed fresh berries (blueberries, raspberries, strawberries)
- 1 tsp chia seeds (optional)

Procedure:

1. Divide the cottage cheese into two bowls.
2. Top each bowl with mixed fresh berries and chia seeds if using.
3. Serve immediately.

Nutritional Values (Per Serving):

- Calories: 150
- Carbohydrates: 12g
- Protein: 15g

- Fat: 5g
- Fiber: 3g
- Sugar: 7g

Cooking Tips:

For added flavor, you can sprinkle some cinnamon or drizzle a bit of honey over the cottage cheese. Choose full-fat cottage cheese for a creamier texture.

Health Benefits:

Cottage cheese is an excellent source of protein and calcium, supporting muscle health and bone strength. Berries are rich in antioxidants and fiber, helping to manage blood sugar levels.

Cucumber Slices with Hummus

This light and refreshing snack pairs crisp cucumber slices with creamy hummus for a perfect balance of hydration, fiber, and plant-based protein.

Time of Preparation: 5 minutes
Cooking Time: None
Serving Units: 2 servings

Ingredients:

- 1 large cucumber, sliced
- 1/4 cup hummus (store-bought or homemade)
- A sprinkle of paprika (optional)

Procedure:

1. Slice the cucumber into rounds or sticks.
2. Serve with hummus on the side for dipping.
3. Optionally, sprinkle paprika or cumin on the hummus for added flavor.

Nutritional Values (Per Serving):

- Calories: 100
- Carbohydrates: 10g
- Protein: 4g
- Fat: 6g
- Fiber: 3g
- Sugar: 2g

Cooking Tips:

For extra crunch, add a few carrot or bell pepper sticks. You can make your own hummus by blending chickpeas, tahini, olive oil, garlic, lemon juice, and spices.

Health Benefits:

Cucumber is low in calories and high in water content, making it a hydrating snack. Hummus provides plant-based protein, fiber, and healthy fats that help regulate blood sugar levels.

Chapter 5

Hearty Soups and Stews

Slow-Cooker Chicken and Vegetable Stew

A comforting and hearty slow-cooked stew packed with tender chicken, nutrient-rich vegetables, and flavorful herbs. This stew is ideal for meal prep or a cozy dinner.

Time of Preparation: 10 minutes

Cooking Time: 6 hours (slow-cooker)

Serving Units: 6 servings

Ingredients:

- 2 boneless, skinless chicken breasts
- 4 cups low-sodium chicken broth
- 2 carrots, peeled and sliced
- 2 celery stalks, sliced
- 1 large onion, diced
- 2 cloves garlic, minced
- 1 cup diced tomatoes
- 1 cup green beans, trimmed
- 1 tsp dried thyme
- 1 tsp dried rosemary
- Salt and pepper to taste
- 1 tbsp olive oil
- Fresh parsley for garnish (optional)

Procedure:

1. In a slow cooker, combine the chicken, chicken broth, carrots, celery, onion, garlic, tomatoes, and green beans.
2. Add the thyme, rosemary, salt, and pepper. Drizzle with olive oil.
3. Set the slow cooker on low heat and cook for 6 hours.
4. Once cooked, shred the chicken using two forks and stir it back into the stew.
5. Serve hot, garnished with fresh parsley if desired.

Nutritional Values (Per Serving):

- Calories: 220
- Carbohydrates: 15g

- Protein: 25g
- Fat: 7g
- Fiber: 4g
- Sugar: 4g

Cooking Tips:

For added flavor, sear the chicken in olive oil before adding it to the slow cooker. You can also substitute chicken thighs for a richer taste.

Health Benefits:

This stew is packed with lean protein from chicken and fiber-rich vegetables, making it perfect for maintaining stable blood sugar levels. It's a satisfying meal for anyone looking to manage their weight or diabetes.

Creamy Cauliflower Soup (Low-Carb)

A rich and creamy soup made with roasted cauliflower, this low-carb dish is blended to perfection for a smooth, velvety texture without the use of heavy cream.

Time of Preparation: 10 minutes

Cooking Time: 30 minutes

Serving Units: 4 servings

Ingredients:

- 1 large head of cauliflower, cut into florets
- 4 cups low-sodium vegetable broth
- 1 onion, diced
- 2 cloves garlic, minced
- 1/2 cup unsweetened almond milk
- 1 tbsp olive oil
- Salt and pepper to taste
- 1/4 tsp nutmeg (optional)
- Fresh parsley or chives for garnish

Procedure:

1. Preheat the oven to 400°F (200°C). Toss the cauliflower florets with olive oil, salt, and pepper. Roast for 20 minutes or until golden.
2. In a large pot, sauté the onion and garlic in olive oil for 5 minutes until softened.
3. Add the roasted cauliflower and vegetable broth to the pot. Simmer for 10 minutes.
4. Blend the soup using an immersion blender or transfer to a blender and puree until smooth.
5. Stir in the almond milk and nutmeg. Adjust seasoning if necessary.
6. Serve hot, garnished with parsley or chives.

Nutritional Values (Per Serving):

- Calories: 120
- Carbohydrates: 12g
- Protein: 4g
- Fat: 6g

- Fiber: 5g
- Sugar: 3g

Cooking Tips:

For a richer flavor, you can add a handful of shredded cheese or a dollop of Greek yogurt. If you like a bit of spice, add a pinch of cayenne pepper.

Health Benefits:

Cauliflower is low in carbohydrates and high in fiber, making this soup a great choice for managing blood sugar. The almond milk keeps the dish creamy without adding excess fat or carbs.

Lentil and Spinach Soup

A hearty, plant-based soup loaded with lentils, fresh spinach, and a blend of aromatic spices. This soup is high in fiber and protein, making it both filling and nourishing.

Time of Preparation: 10 minutes
Cooking Time: 30 minutes
Serving Units: 4 servings

Ingredients:

- 1 cup dried green or brown lentils, rinsed
- 4 cups low-sodium vegetable broth
- 1 onion, diced
- 2 carrots, diced
- 2 cloves garlic, minced
- 1 tsp cumin
- 1/2 tsp turmeric
- 4 cups fresh spinach
- 1 tbsp olive oil
- Salt and pepper to taste
- Lemon wedges for serving

Procedure:

1. In a large pot, heat the olive oil over medium heat. Add the onion, garlic, and carrots, and sauté for 5 minutes until softened.
2. Stir in the cumin and turmeric, cooking for 1 minute until fragrant.
3. Add the lentils and vegetable broth to the pot. Bring to a boil, then reduce heat and simmer for 25–30 minutes, or until the lentils are tender.
4. Stir in the spinach and cook for an additional 2–3 minutes until wilted.
5. Serve hot with a squeeze of lemon juice.

Nutritional Values (Per Serving):

- Calories: 210
- Carbohydrates: 35g
- Protein: 12g
- Fat: 4g
- Fiber: 12g
- Sugar: 4g

Cooking Tips:

For a thicker texture, use an immersion blender

to partially puree the soup. You can also add diced tomatoes for a richer broth.

Health Benefits:

Lentils are packed with plant-based protein and fiber, making this soup ideal for blood sugar regulation. Spinach adds essential vitamins and minerals, including iron and vitamin K.

Butternut Squash Soup with Sage

This creamy butternut squash soup is infused with the earthy flavor of fresh sage and is naturally sweet, making it a perfect choice for a light but hearty meal.

Time of Preparation: 10 minutes

Cooking Time: 30 minutes

Serving Units: 4 servings

Ingredients:

- 1 medium butternut squash, peeled, seeded, and cubed
- 4 cups low-sodium vegetable broth
- 1 onion, diced
- 2 cloves garlic, minced
- 1 tbsp fresh sage, chopped (or 1 tsp dried)
- 1 tbsp olive oil
- Salt and pepper to taste
- 1/4 tsp cinnamon (optional)

Procedure:

1. In a large pot, heat the olive oil over medium heat. Add the onion and garlic, and sauté for 5 minutes until softened.
2. Add the butternut squash and vegetable broth to the pot. Bring to a boil, then reduce heat and simmer for 25 minutes, or until the squash is tender.
3. Stir in the sage and cinnamon if using.
4. Use an immersion blender to puree the soup until smooth.
5. Season with salt and pepper to taste and serve hot.

Nutritional Values (Per Serving):

- Calories: 160
- Carbohydrates: 24g
- Protein: 3g
- Fat: 5g
- Fiber: 4g
- Sugar: 8g

Cooking Tips:

For a richer flavor, roast the butternut squash before adding it to the soup. You can also add a swirl of coconut milk or Greek yogurt for creaminess.

Health Benefits:

Butternut squash is rich in vitamins A and C, along with fiber, which supports healthy digestion and blood sugar control. The sage adds an aromatic touch and contains anti-inflammatory properties.

Beef and Barley Soup

A hearty and filling soup featuring tender beef, fiber-rich barley, and an assortment of vegetables. This soup makes for a satisfying meal that's packed with nutrients.

Time of Preparation: 15 minutes

Cooking Time: 1 hour

Serving Units: 6 servings

Ingredients:

- 1 lb lean beef stew meat, cut into small cubes
- 6 cups low-sodium beef broth
- 1/2 cup pearl barley
- 2 carrots, diced
- 2 celery stalks, diced
- 1 onion, diced
- 2 cloves garlic, minced
- 1 bay leaf
- 1 tsp dried thyme
- 1 tbsp olive oil
- Salt and pepper to taste

Procedure:

1. In a large pot, heat the olive oil over medium-high heat. Add the beef and sear on all sides, about 5 minutes.
2. Add the onion, garlic, carrots, and celery to the pot. Cook for 5 minutes until softened.
3. Stir in the barley, beef broth, bay leaf, thyme, salt, and pepper.
4. Bring to a boil, then reduce heat and simmer for 50–60 minutes, or until the beef is tender and the barley is cooked.
5. Discard the bay leaf and serve hot.

Nutritional Values (Per Serving):

- Calories: 300
- Carbohydrates: 30g
- Protein: 25g
- Fat: 10g
- Fiber: 7g
- Sugar: 4g

Cooking Tips:

You can prepare this soup in a slow cooker by cooking on low for 6–8 hours. Add more vegetables like mushrooms or potatoes for additional heartiness.

Health Benefits:

Barley is a whole grain that provides fiber and complex carbohydrates, making this soup great for stabilizing blood sugar levels. Lean beef offers high-quality protein and essential nutrients like iron.

Turkey and Black Bean Chili

A robust and flavorful chili made with lean ground turkey, black beans, and a medley of spices. This high-protein, fiber-rich dish is perfect for a comforting and filling lunch or dinner.

Time of Preparation: 10 minutes
Cooking Time: 30 minutes
Serving Units: 6 servings

Ingredients:

- 1 lb lean ground turkey
- 1 can (15 oz) black beans, drained and rinsed
- 1 can (15 oz) diced tomatoes
- 1 onion, diced
- 1 bell pepper, diced
- 2 cloves garlic, minced
- 2 tbsp chili powder
- 1 tsp cumin
- 1 tsp smoked paprika
- 1 cup low-sodium chicken broth
- 1 tbsp olive oil
- Salt and pepper to taste
- Fresh cilantro for garnish (optional)

Procedure:

1. Heat the olive oil in a large pot over medium heat. Add the ground turkey and cook until browned, about 5–7 minutes.

2. Add the onion, garlic, and bell pepper to the pot. Cook for 5 minutes until softened.

3. Stir in the chili powder, cumin, smoked paprika, salt, and pepper. Cook for 1 minute.

4. Add the diced tomatoes, black beans, and chicken broth. Bring to a boil, then reduce heat and simmer for 20 minutes.

5. Serve hot, garnished with fresh cilantro if desired.

Nutritional Values (Per Serving):

- Calories: 240
- Carbohydrates: 20g
- Protein: 25g
- Fat: 8g
- Fiber: 8g
- Sugar: 6g

Cooking Tips:

For extra flavor, add a bit of dark chocolate or a splash of lime juice to the chili. You can also top with avocado, sour cream, or shredded cheese.

Health Benefits:

Turkey is a lean protein that helps build muscle and keep you full, while black beans are rich in fiber and antioxidants, making this chili a healthy, diabetes-friendly option.

Chapter 6

Satisfying Dinners

Baked Herb-Crusted Tilapia with Steamed Veggies

A light and flavorful dinner option, tilapia fillets are coated in a blend of herbs and breadcrumbs, then baked to perfection. Served with steamed veggies, this dish is simple yet satisfying.

Time of Preparation: 10 minutes

Cooking Time: 15 minutes

Serving Units: 4 servings

Ingredients:

- 4 tilapia fillets
- 1/2 cup whole wheat breadcrumbs
- 2 tbsp fresh parsley, chopped
- 1 tbsp fresh thyme, chopped
- 1 tbsp lemon zest
- 2 tbsp olive oil
- Salt and pepper to taste
- 1 cup broccoli florets (steamed)
- 1 cup carrots, sliced and steamed

Procedure:

1. Preheat the oven to 400°F (200°C).
2. In a bowl, mix the breadcrumbs, parsley, thyme, lemon zest, olive oil, salt, and pepper.
3. Press the herb mixture onto each tilapia fillet, coating both sides evenly.
4. Place the fillets on a baking sheet lined with parchment paper and bake for 12–15 minutes, or until the fish flakes easily with a fork.
5. Serve with steamed broccoli and carrots.

Nutritional Values (Per Serving):

- Calories: 260
- Carbohydrates: 12g
- Protein: 28g
- Fat: 11g
- Fiber: 4g

- Sugar: 2g

Cooking Tips:

For extra flavor, drizzle the fish with lemon juice before serving. You can also swap tilapia for cod or haddock.

Health Benefits:

Tilapia is a lean source of protein, while the herbs provide antioxidants. Paired with steamed veggies, this dish offers a balanced meal that helps maintain blood sugar levels.

Grilled Chicken with Roasted Brussels Sprouts

Juicy grilled chicken breast paired with crispy roasted Brussels sprouts makes for a simple yet wholesome dinner. This dish is full of flavor and easy to prepare.

Time of Preparation: 10 minutes

Cooking Time: 25 minutes

Serving Units: 4 servings

Ingredients:

- 4 boneless, skinless chicken breasts
- 2 tbsp olive oil
- 2 tsp garlic powder
- 1 tsp paprika
- Salt and pepper to taste
- 4 cups Brussels sprouts, halved
- 1 tbsp balsamic vinegar
- 1 tbsp olive oil

Procedure:

1. Preheat the oven to 400°F (200°C). Toss the Brussels sprouts with olive oil, salt, pepper, and balsamic vinegar. Roast for 20–25 minutes until crispy.
2. Meanwhile, heat a grill pan over medium heat. Season the chicken breasts with garlic powder, paprika, salt, and pepper.
3. Grill the chicken for 5–7 minutes on each side, or until fully cooked and charred.
4. Serve the grilled chicken with roasted Brussels sprouts.

Nutritional Values (Per Serving):

- Calories: 300
- Carbohydrates: 10g

- Protein: 32g
- Fat: 14g
- Fiber: 5g
- Sugar: 4g

Cooking Tips:

For extra flavor, marinate the chicken in olive oil, lemon juice, and herbs for 30 minutes before grilling. Add some roasted sweet potatoes for a heartier meal.

Health Benefits:

Grilled chicken is a great source of lean protein, while Brussels sprouts are rich in fiber and vitamin C, supporting both digestion and immune health.

Spaghetti Squash with Marinara Sauce

A low-carb alternative to traditional pasta, spaghetti squash is paired with a rich marinara sauce for a guilt-free, satisfying dinner.

Time of Preparation: 10 minutes
Cooking Time: 40 minutes
Serving Units: 4 servings

Ingredients:

- 1 large spaghetti squash
- 2 cups marinara sauce (sugar-free)
- 2 tbsp olive oil
- 1 clove garlic, minced
- 1 tsp dried oregano
- Salt and pepper to taste
- Fresh basil for garnish

Procedure:

1. Preheat the oven to 400°F (200°C). Cut the spaghetti squash in half lengthwise, scoop out the seeds, and drizzle with olive oil, salt, and pepper.
2. Place the squash cut side down on a baking sheet and roast for 35–40 minutes until tender.
3. In a saucepan, heat olive oil over medium heat. Add the garlic and sauté until fragrant. Stir in the marinara sauce and oregano, and simmer for 5 minutes.
4. Once the squash is done, scrape out the strands with a fork and toss them with the marinara sauce.
5. Serve hot, garnished with fresh basil.

Nutritional Values (Per Serving):

- Calories: 180
- Carbohydrates: 25g
- Protein: 4g
- Fat: 8g
- Fiber: 5g
- Sugar: 9g

Cooking Tips:

For extra protein, add some grilled chicken or turkey meatballs. You can also sprinkle Parmesan cheese on top for added flavor.

Health Benefits:

Spaghetti squash is low in carbs and high in fiber, making it a great choice for blood sugar management. The marinara sauce provides antioxidants from tomatoes, supporting heart health.

Lemon Garlic Shrimp and Broccoli Stir-Fry

A quick and flavorful stir-fry featuring succulent shrimp and crisp broccoli, tossed in a light lemon garlic sauce. This low-carb meal is perfect for a busy weeknight dinner.

Time of Preparation: 10 minutes

Cooking Time: 10 minutes

Serving Units: 4 servings

Ingredients:

- 1 lb large shrimp, peeled and deveined
- 2 cups broccoli florets
- 2 tbsp olive oil
- 2 cloves garlic, minced
- Juice of 1 lemon
- 1 tbsp soy sauce (low sodium)
- 1/2 tsp red pepper flakes (optional)
- Salt and pepper to taste

Procedure:

1. Heat olive oil in a large skillet over medium-high heat. Add the shrimp and cook for 2–3 minutes per side until pink and opaque. Remove from the skillet and set aside.
2. In the same skillet, add garlic and broccoli, sautéing for 5 minutes until the broccoli is tender.
3. Return the shrimp to the skillet and stir in lemon juice, soy sauce, red pepper flakes, salt, and pepper. Cook for 1 minute.
4. Serve immediately.

Nutritional Values (Per Serving):

- Calories: 220
- Carbohydrates: 7g
- Protein: 28g
- Fat: 10g
- Fiber: 3g
- Sugar: 2g

Cooking Tips:

For more crunch, you can add bell peppers or snap peas to the stir-fry. Serve over cauliflower rice for a low-carb side.

Health Benefits:

Shrimp is an excellent source of lean protein and omega-3 fatty acids, which support heart health. Broccoli is loaded with vitamins, fiber, and antioxidants, making this a nutritious meal for blood sugar control.

Baked Turkey Meatballs with Zoodles

Lean turkey meatballs served over zucchini noodles (zoodles) create a delicious and satisfying low-carb dinner packed with protein and vegetables.

Time of Preparation: 10 minutes

Cooking Time: 20 minutes

Serving Units: 4 servings

Ingredients:

- 1 lb ground turkey (lean)
- 1/4 cup almond flour
- 1 egg
- 2 cloves garlic, minced
- 1 tsp Italian seasoning
- Salt and pepper to taste
- 2 large zucchinis, spiralized
- 1 tbsp olive oil
- 1/2 cup marinara sauce (sugar-free)

Procedure:

1. Preheat the oven to 375°F (190°C).
2. In a large bowl, mix the ground turkey, almond flour, egg, garlic, Italian seasoning, salt, and pepper. Form into small meatballs and place on a baking sheet.
3. Bake for 15–20 minutes until cooked through.
4. Meanwhile, heat olive oil in a skillet over medium heat. Add the zucchini noodles and sauté for 2–3 minutes until just tender.
5. Serve the meatballs over the zoodles, topped with marinara sauce.

Nutritional Values (Per Serving):

- Calories: 290
- Carbohydrates: 10g
- Protein: 30g
- Fat: 15g
- Fiber: 4g
- Sugar: 3g

Cooking Tips:

For extra flavor, add grated Parmesan cheese or fresh basil to the meatballs. You can also make a double batch and freeze some for later use.

Health Benefits:

Turkey is a lean protein source, while zucchini noodles provide a low-carb alternative to pasta, helping to manage blood sugar levels. Almond flour adds healthy fats and fiber.

Pork Tenderloin with Sautéed Spinach

Juicy pork tenderloin served with nutrient-dense sautéed spinach makes for a wholesome and satisfying dinner that's rich in protein and low in carbs.

Time of Preparation: 10 minutes
Cooking Time: 20 minutes
Serving Units: 4 servings

Ingredients:

- 1 lb pork tenderloin
- 2 tbsp olive oil
- 2 cloves garlic, minced
- 4 cups fresh spinach
- 1 tbsp balsamic vinegar
- Salt and pepper to taste
- 1 tsp dried rosemary

Procedure:

1. Preheat the oven to 400°F (200°C).
2. Season the pork tenderloin with salt, pepper, and rosemary. Heat 1 tbsp olive oil in an oven-safe skillet over medium-high heat and sear the pork on all sides.
3. Transfer the skillet to the oven and roast for 15–20 minutes, or until the internal temperature reaches 145°F (63°C). Let the pork rest for 5 minutes before slicing.
4. In a separate skillet, heat the remaining olive oil over medium heat. Add garlic and sauté until fragrant, then add the spinach and cook until wilted, about 2 minutes.
5. Drizzle the spinach with balsamic vinegar and serve alongside the sliced pork tenderloin.

Nutritional Values (Per Serving):

- Calories: 320
- Carbohydrates: 5g
- Protein: 36g
- Fat: 18g
- Fiber: 2g
- Sugar: 2g

Cooking Tips:

For extra flavor, marinate the pork in a mixture of olive oil, garlic, and rosemary for a few hours before cooking. You can also add mushrooms to the spinach for more texture.

Chapter 7

Tasty Vegetarian Options

Eggplant Lasagna (Low-Carb)

This low-carb lasagna uses thin slices of eggplant in place of pasta for a healthy twist on a classic dish. Layered with ricotta, marinara, and mozzarella, it's a satisfying vegetarian meal.

Time of Preparation: 15 minutes

Cooking Time: 40 minutes

Serving Units: 4 servings

Ingredients:

- 2 large eggplants, sliced lengthwise into thin strips
- 2 cups ricotta cheese
- 1/2 cup grated Parmesan cheese
- 1 cup shredded mozzarella cheese
- 2 cups marinara sauce (sugar-free)
- 1 egg
- 1 tbsp olive oil
- Salt and pepper to taste
- Fresh basil for garnish

Procedure:

1. Preheat the oven to 375°F (190°C). Sprinkle salt on the eggplant slices and let them sit for 15 minutes to draw out moisture. Rinse and pat dry.
2. In a bowl, mix the ricotta, egg, Parmesan, salt, and pepper.
3. Heat olive oil in a pan over medium heat and grill the eggplant slices for 2-3 minutes on each side until tender.
4. In a baking dish, spread a thin layer of marinara sauce. Add a layer of eggplant slices, followed by the ricotta mixture, and a sprinkle of mozzarella.
5. Repeat the layers, ending with marinara and mozzarella on top.

6. Bake for 30-35 minutes until the cheese is bubbly and golden. Garnish with fresh basil and serve.

Nutritional Values (Per Serving):

- Calories: 280
- Carbohydrates: 12g
- Protein: 18g
- Fat: 18g
- Fiber: 6g
- Sugar: 8g

Cooking Tips:

To avoid excess moisture, pat the eggplant slices dry after salting. You can also add some spinach or mushrooms to the ricotta mixture for extra flavor.

Health Benefits:

Eggplant is low in carbs and high in fiber, making this lasagna perfect for managing blood sugar. Ricotta and mozzarella provide protein and calcium.

Stuffed Portobello Mushrooms with Quinoa

Hearty portobello mushrooms are stuffed with a flavorful quinoa and vegetable mixture, then baked until tender. This protein-packed vegetarian dish is both filling and nutritious.

Time of Preparation: 10 minutes
Cooking Time: 20 minutes
Serving Units: 4 servings

Ingredients:

- 4 large portobello mushrooms, stems removed
- 1 cup cooked quinoa
- 1/4 cup diced red bell pepper
- 1/4 cup diced onion
- 1 clove garlic, minced
- 1 tbsp olive oil
- 1 tbsp fresh parsley, chopped
- 2 tbsp grated Parmesan cheese
- Salt and pepper to taste

Procedure:

1. Preheat the oven to 375°F (190°C). Brush the portobello mushrooms with olive oil and place them on a baking sheet.
2. In a skillet, heat olive oil and sauté the onion, garlic, and red bell pepper until softened. Stir in the cooked quinoa, parsley, salt, and pepper.
3. Stuff the mushroom caps with the quinoa mixture and sprinkle with Parmesan cheese.
4. Bake for 15-20 minutes, or until the mushrooms are tender and the tops are golden brown.

5. Serve hot.

Nutritional Values (Per Serving):

- Calories: 220
- Carbohydrates: 25g
- Protein: 8g
- Fat: 9g
- Fiber: 5g
- Sugar: 3g

Cooking Tips:

You can customize the stuffing by adding spinach, sun-dried tomatoes, or crumbled feta. For a vegan version, skip the Parmesan or use a plant-based cheese.

Health Benefits:

Portobello mushrooms are a low-calorie, fiber-rich food, and quinoa is a complete protein that supports muscle health and digestion.

Grilled Tofu with Asian Vegetables

This grilled tofu dish is paired with a medley of colorful Asian-inspired vegetables and a light soy-ginger sauce, creating a well-balanced, protein-rich vegetarian dinner.

Time of Preparation: 10 minutes

Cooking Time: 15 minutes

Serving Units: 4 servings

Ingredients:

- 1 block firm tofu, pressed and sliced
- 1 tbsp soy sauce (low sodium)
- 1 tsp sesame oil
- 1 clove garlic, minced
- 1 tsp fresh ginger, grated
- 1 red bell pepper, sliced
- 1 cup broccoli florets
- 1/2 cup snap peas
- 1 tbsp olive oil
- Sesame seeds for garnish
- Fresh cilantro for garnish

Procedure:

1. In a small bowl, mix the soy sauce, sesame oil, garlic, and ginger. Marinate the tofu slices for 10 minutes.
2. Heat a grill pan over medium heat and grill the tofu for 3-4 minutes per side until golden and charred. Remove and set aside.
3. In a skillet, heat olive oil over medium heat and stir-fry the bell pepper, broccoli, and snap peas for 5-6 minutes until tender-crisp.
4. Serve the grilled tofu on a bed of vegetables, garnished with sesame seeds and cilantro.

Nutritional Values (Per Serving):

- Calories: 250
- Carbohydrates: 12g
- Protein: 18g
- Fat: 14g
- Fiber: 5g
- Sugar: 4g

Cooking Tips:

Press the tofu for at least 20 minutes before grilling to remove excess moisture. For a spicier flavor, add a pinch of red pepper flakes to the marinade.

Health Benefits:

Tofu is a plant-based protein rich in essential amino acids, and the vegetables provide fiber, vitamins, and antioxidants for a well-rounded meal.

Sweet Potato and Black Bean Tacos

These hearty tacos are filled with roasted sweet potatoes, black beans, and a zesty lime dressing, offering a flavorful and nutrient-packed vegetarian option.

Time of Preparation: 10 minutes

Cooking Time: 20 minutes

Serving Units: 4 servings (8 tacos)

Ingredients:

- 2 medium sweet potatoes, peeled and diced
- 1 can (15 oz) black beans, rinsed and drained
- 8 small corn tortillas
- 2 tbsp olive oil
- 1 tsp cumin
- 1 tsp smoked paprika
- Salt and pepper to taste
- 1/4 cup fresh cilantro, chopped
- 1 lime, cut into wedges
- Optional toppings: avocado, salsa, shredded lettuce

Procedure:

1. Preheat the oven to 400°F (200°C). Toss the diced sweet potatoes with olive oil, cumin, smoked paprika, salt, and pepper. Roast for 20 minutes or until tender.
2. Heat the black beans in a small saucepan over medium heat.
3. Warm the tortillas in a dry skillet or microwave.
4. Assemble the tacos by adding a scoop of roasted sweet potatoes and black beans to each tortilla. Top with cilantro and a squeeze of lime.
5. Serve with optional toppings like avocado or salsa.

Nutritional Values (Per Serving):

- Calories: 300
- Carbohydrates: 50g
- Protein: 9g
- Fat: 8g
- Fiber: 10g
- Sugar: 7g

Cooking Tips:

For added flavor, drizzle the tacos with a creamy lime-cilantro dressing made with Greek yogurt, lime juice, and cilantro.

Health Benefits:

Sweet potatoes are rich in fiber, vitamins A and C, and black beans provide protein and fiber, making these tacos a nutrient-dense option that helps stabilize blood sugar.

Cauliflower Rice Stir-Fry

A low-carb, veggie-packed stir-fry featuring cauliflower rice, crisp vegetables, and a light soy-ginger sauce. This quick and easy dinner is perfect for busy weeknights.

Time of Preparation: 10 minutes
Cooking Time: 10 minutes
Serving Units: 4 servings

Ingredients:

- 4 cups cauliflower rice
- 1 cup carrots, julienned
- 1 cup peas
- 1 red bell pepper, diced
- 2 green onions, chopped
- 2 tbsp soy sauce (low sodium)
- 1 tsp sesame oil
- 1 clove garlic, minced
- 1 tsp fresh ginger, grated
- 1 tbsp olive oil
- Sesame seeds for garnish

Procedure:

1. Heat olive oil in a large skillet over medium heat. Add the garlic and ginger and sauté for 1 minute until fragrant.
2. Add the carrots, peas, and bell pepper, and stir-fry for 3-4 minutes until tender.

3. Stir in the cauliflower rice and soy sauce, and cook for another 2-3 minutes until heated through.
4. Drizzle with sesame oil and top with green onions and sesame seeds. Serve hot.

Nutritional Values (Per Serving):

- Calories: 150
- Carbohydrates: 18g
- Protein: 5g
- Fat: 7g
- Fiber: 5g
- Sugar: 6g

Cooking Tips:

Use pre-packaged cauliflower rice for convenience, or make your own by pulsing cauliflower florets in a food processor. You can add tofu or tempeh for extra protein.

Health Benefits:

Cauliflower is low in carbs and high in fiber, while the mixed vegetables provide essential vitamins and minerals. This stir-fry is a great option for weight management and blood sugar control.

6. Baked Falafel with Cucumber Salad

Crispy baked falafel made with chickpeas, herbs, and spices, served alongside a refreshing cucumber salad. This healthy vegetarian dish is packed with flavor and nutrients.

Time of Preparation: 15 minutes
Cooking Time: 20 minutes
Serving Units: 4 servings

Ingredients:

- 1 can (15 oz) chickpeas, drained and rinsed
- 1/4 cup fresh parsley
- 1/4 cup fresh cilantro
- 1/2 red onion, chopped
- 2 cloves garlic, minced
- 2 tbsp olive oil
- 1 tsp cumin
- 1 tsp coriander
- Salt and pepper to taste
- 1/4 cup whole wheat flour
- 1 cucumber, sliced
- 1 tbsp lemon juice
- 1 tbsp olive oil

Procedure:

1. Preheat the oven to 375°F (190°C). In a food processor, combine the chickpeas, parsley, cilantro, onion, garlic, cumin, coriander, salt, and pepper. Pulse until the mixture is coarse and holds together.
2. Stir in the flour to form a dough. Shape the mixture into small patties and place on a baking sheet.
3. Brush the patties with olive oil and bake for 15-20 minutes, flipping halfway through, until golden and crispy.
4. Meanwhile, toss the cucumber slices with lemon juice, olive oil, salt, and pepper.
5. Serve the falafel with cucumber salad.

Nutritional Values (Per Serving):

- Calories: 250
- Carbohydrates: 30g
- Protein: 8g
- Fat: 10g
- Fiber: 8g
- Sugar: 3g

Cooking Tips:

For extra crispiness, finish the falafel under the broiler for 1-2 minutes. Serve with a side of hummus or tzatziki for added flavor.

Health Benefits:

Chickpeas are a great source of plant-based protein and fiber, which aid in digestion and blood sugar control. The cucumber salad adds hydration and antioxidants to the meal.

Chapter 8

Flavorful Fish and Seafood

Lemon Baked Cod with Asparagus

A simple yet flavorful dish where tender cod fillets are baked with fresh lemon juice and garlic, served with roasted asparagus for a light, nutrient-packed meal.

Time of Preparation: 10 minutes
Cooking Time: 15 minutes
Serving Units: 4 servings

Ingredients:

- 4 cod fillets
- 1 bunch asparagus, trimmed
- 2 tbsp olive oil
- 2 cloves garlic, minced
- Juice of 1 lemon
- Salt and pepper to taste
- Fresh parsley for garnish

Procedure:

1. Preheat the oven to 400°F (200°C).
2. Place the cod fillets on a baking sheet lined with parchment paper. Arrange the asparagus around the fish.
3. Drizzle olive oil over the fish and asparagus, then sprinkle with garlic, lemon juice, salt, and pepper.
4. Bake for 12–15 minutes, or until the cod is cooked through and flakes easily with a fork.
5. Garnish with fresh parsley and serve.

Nutritional Values (Per Serving):

- Calories: 220
- Carbohydrates: 5g
- Protein: 28g
- Fat: 9g
- Fiber: 3g
- Sugar: 2g

Cooking Tips:

For extra flavor, marinate the cod in lemon juice and garlic for 30 minutes before baking. You can also add cherry tomatoes for a burst of color and sweetness.

Health Benefits:

Cod is a lean source of protein and low in fat, making it ideal for heart health. Asparagus is rich in fiber, folate, and vitamins A, C, and K.

Grilled Mahi-Mahi with Pineapple Salsa

Grilled mahi-mahi fillets are paired with a sweet and tangy pineapple salsa, creating a refreshing and tropical seafood dish that's both light and flavorful.

Time of Preparation: 15 minutes
Cooking Time: 10 minutes
Serving Units: 4 servings

Ingredients:

- 4 mahi-mahi fillets
- 2 tbsp olive oil
- 1/2 tsp cumin
- Salt and pepper to taste

For Pineapple Salsa:

- 1 cup fresh pineapple, diced
- 1/4 cup red onion, diced
- 1/2 jalapeño, seeded and minced
- 1/4 cup fresh cilantro, chopped
- Juice of 1 lime
- Salt to taste

Procedure:

1. Preheat a grill or grill pan over medium-high heat. Rub the mahi-mahi fillets with olive oil, cumin, salt, and pepper.
2. Grill the fillets for 3-4 minutes per side, or until the fish is fully cooked and has nice grill marks.
3. In a bowl, combine all the salsa ingredients and mix well.
4. Serve the grilled mahi-mahi with pineapple salsa on top.

Nutritional Values (Per Serving):

- Calories: 250
- Carbohydrates: 12g
- Protein: 30g

- Fat: 10g
- Fiber: 3g
- Sugar: 8g

Cooking Tips:

For added sweetness, you can grill the pineapple before making the salsa. Serve with a side of cauliflower rice for a low-carb meal.

Health Benefits:

Mahi-mahi is a lean, protein-rich fish that provides omega-3 fatty acids, while pineapple adds vitamin C and digestive enzymes.

Shrimp Skewers with Zucchini and Bell Peppers

Juicy shrimp are skewered with zucchini and bell peppers, then grilled to perfection for a healthy, colorful, and flavorful seafood dish.

Time of Preparation: 10 minutes
Cooking Time: 10 minutes
Serving Units: 4 servings

Ingredients:

- 1 lb large shrimp, peeled and deveined
- 2 zucchinis, sliced
- 1 red bell pepper, cut into squares
- 1 yellow bell pepper, cut into squares
- 2 tbsp olive oil
- 1 tsp paprika
- 1 clove garlic, minced
- Salt and pepper to taste
- Lemon wedges for serving

Procedure:

1. Preheat the grill to medium heat. Thread the shrimp, zucchini, and bell peppers onto skewers.
2. In a small bowl, mix the olive oil, paprika, garlic, salt, and pepper. Brush the skewers with the olive oil mixture.
3. Grill the skewers for 2-3 minutes per side, or until the shrimp are pink and cooked through.
4. Serve with lemon wedges.

Nutritional Values (Per Serving):

- Calories: 210
- Carbohydrates: 6g
- Protein: 26g
- Fat: 10g
- Fiber: 2g
- Sugar: 3g

Cooking Tips:

Soak wooden skewers in water for 30 minutes before grilling to prevent them from burning. You can also add mushrooms or cherry tomatoes to the skewers for extra variety.

Health Benefits:

Shrimp is a low-calorie, high-protein seafood option, rich in selenium and antioxidants. The vegetables add fiber and vitamins, making this a balanced meal.

Salmon Cakes with Avocado Salsa

These delicious salmon cakes are pan-seared until golden and served with a creamy avocado salsa, offering a light and protein-packed seafood dinner.

Time of Preparation: 15 minutes
Cooking Time: 10 minutes
Serving Units: 4 servings

Ingredients:

- 2 cups cooked salmon, flaked
- 1/2 cup almond flour
- 1 egg
- 1 tbsp Dijon mustard
- 1 tbsp fresh dill, chopped
- 1/4 cup green onions, chopped
- Salt and pepper to taste
- 2 tbsp olive oil

For Avocado Salsa:

- 1 ripe avocado, diced
- 1/4 cup red onion, diced
- 1 tbsp lime juice
- 1 tbsp fresh cilantro, chopped
- Salt to taste

Procedure:

1. In a bowl, mix the flaked salmon, almond flour, egg, Dijon mustard, dill, green onions, salt, and pepper. Form into small patties.
2. Heat olive oil in a skillet over medium heat. Cook the salmon cakes for 3-4 minutes per side until golden brown.
3. In a separate bowl, combine all the salsa ingredients and mix well.
4. Serve the salmon cakes with avocado salsa on top.

Nutritional Values (Per Serving):

- Calories: 320
- Carbohydrates: 7g
- Protein: 26g
- Fat: 21g
- Fiber: 6g
- Sugar: 2g

Cooking Tips:

For extra flavor, you can add a pinch of cayenne pepper to the salmon mixture. You can also bake the salmon cakes at 375°F (190°C) for 15 minutes instead of pan-frying.

Health Benefits:

Salmon is an excellent source of omega-3 fatty acids, which support heart health. Avocado provides healthy fats and fiber, making this a well-rounded and nutrient-dense meal.

Tuna Salad Lettuce Wraps

Light and refreshing, these tuna salad lettuce wraps are a low-carb and protein-rich option that's perfect for a quick lunch or light dinner.

Time of Preparation: 10 minutes

Cooking Time: None

Serving Units: 4 servings

Ingredients:

- 2 cans (5 oz each) tuna in water, drained
- 1/4 cup Greek yogurt
- 1 tbsp Dijon mustard
- 1 tbsp fresh lemon juice
- 1/4 cup celery, diced
- 2 tbsp red onion, diced
- Salt and pepper to taste
- 8 large lettuce leaves (Romaine or butter lettuce)

Procedure:

1. In a bowl, combine the tuna, Greek yogurt, Dijon mustard, lemon juice, celery, red onion, salt, and pepper. Mix well.
2. Spoon the tuna salad into the center of each lettuce leaf.
3. Roll the lettuce leaves up into wraps and serve immediately.

Nutritional Values (Per Serving):

- Calories: 180
- Carbohydrates: 3g
- Protein: 30g
- Fat: 6g
- Fiber: 1g
- Sugar: 2g

Cooking Tips:

For extra crunch, add some chopped cucumbers or bell peppers to the tuna salad. You can also serve the salad on whole wheat crackers for a different variation.

Health Benefits:

Tuna is a lean source of protein and contains omega-3 fatty acids. The lettuce provides a low-carb, fiber-rich base, making this meal great for managing blood sugar.

Baked Catfish with Cajun Spices

Catfish fillets are coated in a flavorful Cajun spice blend and baked until crispy, creating a satisfying seafood dish with a spicy kick.

Time of Preparation: 10 minutes

Cooking Time: 20 minutes

Serving Units: 4 servings

Ingredients:

- 4 catfish fillets
- 2 tbsp olive oil
- 1 tbsp Cajun seasoning
- 1 tsp paprika
- 1/2 tsp garlic powder
- Salt and pepper to taste
- Lemon wedges for serving

Procedure:

1. Preheat the oven to 375°F (190°C). Line a baking sheet with parchment paper.
2. Brush the catfish fillets with olive oil and sprinkle with Cajun seasoning, paprika, garlic powder, salt, and pepper.
3. Bake for 18-20 minutes, or until the catfish is golden brown and fully cooked.
4. Serve with lemon wedges.

Nutritional Values (Per Serving):

- Calories: 260
- Carbohydrates: 3g
- Protein: 30g
- Fat: 14g
- Fiber: 1g
- Sugar: 0g

Cooking Tips:

For a crispy texture, turn on the broiler for the last 2 minutes of baking. Serve the catfish with a side of steamed vegetables or a simple salad.

Health Benefits:

Catfish is a lean protein source, and the Cajun spices provide antioxidants and anti-inflammatory properties. This dish is low in carbs, making it perfect for managing blood sugar levels.

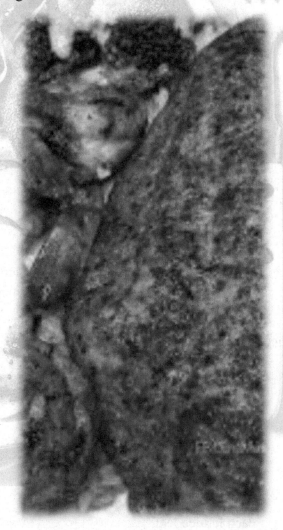

Chapter 9

Low-Carb Sides

Garlic Mashed Cauliflower

A creamy, low-carb alternative to traditional mashed potatoes, this garlic mashed cauliflower is smooth, flavorful, and perfect for pairing with any main course.

Time of Preparation: 10 minutes
Cooking Time: 15 minutes
Serving Units: 4 servings

Ingredients:

- 1 large head of cauliflower, cut into florets
- 3 cloves garlic, minced
- 2 tbsp unsalted butter
- 1/4 cup heavy cream
- Salt and pepper to taste
- Fresh parsley for garnish (optional)

Procedure:

1. Bring a large pot of water to a boil and cook the cauliflower florets for 10-12 minutes until tender.
2. Drain the cauliflower and transfer to a food processor or blender. Add the garlic, butter, heavy cream, salt, and pepper.
3. Blend until smooth and creamy. Adjust seasoning as needed.
4. Serve hot, garnished with fresh parsley if desired.

Nutritional Values (Per Serving):

- Calories: 130
- Carbohydrates: 8g
- Protein: 3g
- Fat: 10g
- Fiber: 3g
- Sugar: 3g

Cooking Tips:

For a richer flavor, you can add a tablespoon of cream cheese to the mix. You can also roast the garlic for a deeper flavor profile.

Health Benefits:

Cauliflower is a low-carb vegetable high in fiber and vitamins C and K. This dish is a satisfying and diabetes-friendly substitute for mashed potatoes.

Roasted Brussels Sprouts with Balsamic Glaze

Crispy roasted Brussels sprouts are drizzled with a sweet and tangy balsamic glaze, making this side dish a flavorful and nutrient-packed addition to any meal.

Time of Preparation: 5 minutes

Cooking Time: 25 minutes

Serving Units: 4 servings

Ingredients:

- 4 cups Brussels sprouts, halved
- 2 tbsp olive oil
- Salt and pepper to taste
- 2 tbsp balsamic vinegar
- 1 tbsp honey (optional)
- 1 tsp Dijon mustard

Procedure:

1. Preheat the oven to 400°F (200°C). Toss the Brussels sprouts with olive oil, salt, and pepper, and spread them in a single layer on a baking sheet.
2. Roast for 20-25 minutes until crispy and golden brown.
3. While the Brussels sprouts are roasting, whisk together balsamic vinegar, honey (if using), and Dijon mustard in a small saucepan. Simmer for 5 minutes until slightly thickened.
4. Drizzle the balsamic glaze over the roasted Brussels sprouts and serve.

Nutritional Values (Per Serving):

- Calories: 160
- Carbohydrates: 12g
- Protein: 4g
- Fat: 10g
- Fiber: 5g
- Sugar: 6g

Cooking Tips:

You can add a handful of toasted walnuts or almonds for extra crunch. If you prefer a more intense balsamic flavor, reduce the glaze a bit longer until it thickens further.

Health Benefits:

Brussels sprouts are high in fiber, antioxidants, and vitamins, particularly vitamin C. The balsamic glaze adds a sweet touch without overloading on sugar.

3. Sautéed Zucchini with Parmesan

Lightly sautéed zucchini topped with grated Parmesan cheese creates a quick, low-carb side dish that's bursting with flavor and texture.

Time of Preparation: 5 minutes
Cooking Time: 8 minutes
Serving Units: 4 servings

Ingredients:

- 4 medium zucchinis, sliced into rounds
- 2 tbsp olive oil
- 2 cloves garlic, minced
- 1/4 cup grated Parmesan cheese
- Salt and pepper to taste
- Fresh basil for garnish (optional)

Procedure:

1. Heat olive oil in a large skillet over medium heat. Add the garlic and sauté for 1 minute until fragrant.
2. Add the zucchini slices and cook for 5-6 minutes, stirring occasionally, until they are tender but still slightly crisp.
3. Season with salt and pepper, then sprinkle with Parmesan cheese.
4. Garnish with fresh basil and serve hot.

Nutritional Values (Per Serving):

- Calories: 140
- Carbohydrates: 6g
- Protein: 5g
- Fat: 11g
- Fiber: 2g
- Sugar: 3g

Cooking Tips:

To prevent the zucchini from becoming too soft, avoid overcrowding the pan and cook in batches if necessary. You can also add a splash of lemon juice for a zesty finish.

Health Benefits:

Zucchini is a low-calorie vegetable high in antioxidants, vitamins, and fiber. The Parmesan adds a bit of protein and calcium, making this dish both tasty and nutritious.

Grilled Asparagus with Lemon Zest

Crisp and tender grilled asparagus spears are lightly seasoned and topped with lemon zest for a bright, refreshing flavor. This simple side dish pairs well with any protein.

Time of Preparation: 5 minutes
Cooking Time: 8 minutes
Serving Units: 4 servings

Ingredients:

- 1 bunch asparagus, trimmed
- 2 tbsp olive oil
- Zest of 1 lemon
- Salt and pepper to taste
- 1 tbsp grated Parmesan (optional)

Procedure:

1. Preheat the grill to medium heat. Toss the asparagus with olive oil, salt, and pepper.
2. Grill the asparagus for 3-4 minutes per side, until tender and slightly charred.
3. Remove from the grill and sprinkle with lemon zest and Parmesan, if desired.
4. Serve immediately.

Nutritional Values (Per Serving):

- Calories: 100
- Carbohydrates: 5g
- Protein: 3g
- Fat: 8g
- Fiber: 3g
- Sugar: 2g

Cooking Tips:

You can also roast the asparagus in the oven at 400°F (200°C) for 12-15 minutes if grilling is not an option. For a more intense lemon flavor, squeeze some fresh lemon juice over the asparagus before serving.

Health Benefits:

Asparagus is low in calories and carbohydrates, making it ideal for weight management and blood sugar control. It is also a good source of vitamins A, C, and K.

Spinach and Feta-Stuffed Mushrooms

Large mushroom caps are filled with a savory mixture of sautéed spinach, garlic, and feta cheese, then baked to perfection. These stuffed mushrooms make a rich yet low-carb side dish.

Time of Preparation: 10 minutes
Cooking Time: 15 minutes
Serving Units: 4 servings

Ingredients:

- 12 large button or cremini mushrooms, stems removed
- 2 cups fresh spinach, chopped
- 1/4 cup feta cheese, crumbled
- 2 cloves garlic, minced
- 1 tbsp olive oil
- Salt and pepper to taste
- 1 tbsp fresh parsley for garnish

Procedure:

1. Preheat the oven to 375°F (190°C). Place the mushroom caps on a baking sheet.
2. Heat olive oil in a skillet over medium heat. Add the garlic and sauté for 1 minute.
3. Add the spinach and cook until wilted, about 2-3 minutes. Stir in the feta cheese, salt, and pepper.
4. Stuff each mushroom cap with the spinach and feta mixture.
5. Bake for 12-15 minutes until the mushrooms are tender.
6. Garnish with parsley and serve.

Nutritional Values (Per Serving):

- Calories: 120
- Carbohydrates: 6g
- Protein: 5g
- Fat: 9g
- Fiber: 2g
- Sugar: 2g

Cooking Tips:

For added texture, sprinkle breadcrumbs on top of the stuffed mushrooms before baking. You can also swap feta with goat cheese for a creamier filling.

Health Benefits:

Mushrooms are low in calories and provide important vitamins and minerals like vitamin D and potassium. Spinach and feta add calcium, fiber, and a boost of antioxidants.

Carrot Fries with Herb Yogurt Dip

These roasted carrot fries are crispy on the outside and tender on the inside, served with a refreshing herb yogurt dip for a healthy and satisfying low-carb side.

Time of Preparation: 10 minutes
Cooking Time: 25 minutes
Serving Units: 4 servings

Ingredients:

- 6 large carrots, peeled and cut into fries
- 2 tbsp olive oil
- 1 tsp smoked paprika
- Salt and pepper to taste

- 1/2 cup plain Greek yogurt
- 1 tbsp fresh dill, chopped
- 1 tbsp fresh parsley, chopped
- 1 tsp lemon juice

Procedure:

1. Preheat the oven to 425°F (220°C). Toss the carrot fries with olive oil, smoked paprika, salt, and pepper, and spread them on a baking sheet.
2. Roast for 20-25 minutes, flipping halfway through, until crispy and golden brown.
3. In a small bowl, mix the Greek yogurt, dill, parsley, and lemon juice. Season with salt and pepper.
4. Serve the carrot fries with the herb yogurt dip on the side.

Nutritional Values (Per Serving):

- Calories: 150
- Carbohydrates: 12g
- Protein: 3g
- Fat: 9g
- Fiber: 4g
- Sugar: 7g

Cooking Tips:

For extra crispiness, use a convection setting on your oven. You can also substitute sweet potatoes for the carrots for a slightly sweeter version of this dish.

Health Benefits:

Carrots are rich in beta-carotene, which supports eye health, and Greek yogurt provides probiotics and protein, making this dish both nutritious and delicious.

Chapter 10

Indulgent Yet Healthy Desserts

Sugar-Free Chocolate Avocado Mousse

Rich and creamy, this chocolate mousse is made with avocados for a healthy twist. It's sugar-free and full of healthy fats, making it a guilt-free indulgence.

Time of Preparation: 5 minutes

Cooking Time: None

Serving Units: 4 servings

Ingredients:

- 2 ripe avocados
- 1/4 cup unsweetened cocoa powder
- 1/4 cup sugar-free sweetener (like stevia or monk fruit)
- 1/4 cup unsweetened almond milk
- 1 tsp vanilla extract
- A pinch of sea salt
- Fresh raspberries for garnish (optional)

Procedure:

1. Scoop the avocados into a blender or food processor. Add the cocoa powder, sweetener, almond milk, vanilla extract, and sea salt.
2. Blend until smooth and creamy.
3. Spoon the mousse into serving dishes and refrigerate for 30 minutes to chill.
4. Garnish with fresh raspberries before serving.

Nutritional Values (Per Serving):

- Calories: 180
- Carbohydrates: 12g
- Protein: 3g
- Fat: 15g
- Fiber: 7g

- Sugar: 1g

Cooking Tips:

For a more intense chocolate flavor, add a tablespoon of sugar-free dark chocolate chips. You can also top with whipped cream or chopped nuts.

Health Benefits:

Avocados are rich in heart-healthy monounsaturated fats and fiber, which support healthy cholesterol levels and digestion. This mousse is low in sugar and packed with healthy fats.

Baked Apples with Cinnamon and Walnuts

A warm, comforting dessert made with baked apples, cinnamon, and crunchy walnuts. This simple dessert is naturally sweet and free of refined sugars.

Time of Preparation: 10 minutes
Cooking Time: 25 minutes
Serving Units: 4 servings

Ingredients:

- 4 medium apples, cored
- 2 tbsp chopped walnuts
- 1 tsp ground cinnamon
- 1 tbsp melted butter
- 1 tsp vanilla extract
- 1 tbsp sugar-free sweetener (optional)

Procedure:

1. Preheat the oven to 350°F (175°C).
2. In a small bowl, mix the chopped walnuts, cinnamon, melted butter, vanilla extract, and sweetener if using.
3. Place the cored apples in a baking dish and stuff the centers with the walnut mixture.
4. Bake for 20-25 minutes until the apples are tender.
5. Serve warm, optionally with a dollop of sugar-free whipped cream.

Nutritional Values (Per Serving):

- Calories: 150
- Carbohydrates: 22g
- Protein: 2g
- Fat: 7g
- Fiber: 5g
- Sugar: 14g

Cooking Tips:

You can add a sprinkle of nutmeg or cloves for extra spice. For added richness, drizzle with a bit of sugar-free caramel sauce before serving.

Health Benefits:

Apples are a good source of fiber and vitamin C, and walnuts add healthy fats and omega-3s, making this dessert both nutritious and satisfying.

Almond Flour Brownies

These fudgy brownies are made with almond flour, making them gluten-free and low in carbs. They're perfect for satisfying your chocolate cravings without the guilt.

Time of Preparation: 10 minutes
Cooking Time: 20 minutes
Serving Units: 12 brownies

Ingredients:

- 1 cup almond flour
- 1/2 cup unsweetened cocoa powder
- 1/2 cup sugar-free sweetener (like erythritol)
- 2 large eggs
- 1/4 cup melted coconut oil
- 1 tsp vanilla extract
- 1/2 tsp baking powder
- A pinch of salt

Procedure:

1. Preheat the oven to 350°F (175°C). Grease an 8x8-inch baking pan or line with parchment paper.
2. In a medium bowl, whisk together the almond flour, cocoa powder, sweetener, baking powder, and salt.
3. Add the eggs, melted coconut oil, and vanilla extract, and stir until well combined.
4. Pour the batter into the prepared baking pan and smooth the top.
5. Bake for 18-20 minutes or until a toothpick inserted in the center comes out clean.
6. Let cool before cutting into squares.

Nutritional Values (Per Serving):

- Calories: 150
- Carbohydrates: 6g
- Protein: 5g
- Fat: 13g
- Fiber: 3g
- Sugar: 1g

Cooking Tips:

For extra indulgence, add sugar-free chocolate chips or chopped nuts to the batter. You can also top the brownies with a drizzle of melted sugar-free chocolate.

Health Benefits:

Almond flour is rich in healthy fats, fiber, and protein, making these brownies a great low-carb alternative to traditional recipes. The sugar-free sweetener keeps blood sugar levels stable.

Coconut Chia Pudding with Raspberries

This creamy coconut chia pudding is rich in fiber and healthy fats. Topped with fresh raspberries, it makes for a light and satisfying dessert.

Time of Preparation: 5 minutes
Chill Time: 4 hours (or overnight)
Serving Units: 4 servings

Ingredients:

- 1/4 cup chia seeds
- 1 cup unsweetened coconut milk
- 1 tbsp sugar-free sweetener (like stevia or monk fruit)
- 1 tsp vanilla extract
- 1/2 cup fresh raspberries for topping

Procedure:

1. In a bowl or jar, combine chia seeds, coconut milk, sweetener, and vanilla extract. Stir well to combine.
2. Cover and refrigerate for at least 4 hours or overnight, stirring once after 1 hour to prevent clumping.
3. When ready to serve, top the pudding with fresh raspberries.

Nutritional Values (Per Serving):

- Calories: 180
- Carbohydrates: 12g
- Protein: 4g
- Fat: 13g
- Fiber: 9g
- Sugar: 3g

Cooking Tips:

For added texture, stir in shredded coconut or sugar-free chocolate chips before chilling. You can also layer the pudding with raspberries for a parfait-style dessert.

Health Benefits:

Chia seeds are an excellent source of omega-3 fatty acids, fiber, and antioxidants. Coconut milk provides healthy fats, making this pudding both delicious and nutritious.

Lemon Cheesecake Bites

These zesty, no-bake lemon cheesecake bites are a delicious and low-carb treat, perfect for a refreshing dessert or snack. They're creamy, tangy, and guilt-free.

Time of Preparation: 10 minutes
Chill Time: 1 hour
Serving Units: 12 bites

Ingredients:

- 1 cup cream cheese, softened
- 1/4 cup sugar-free sweetener (like erythritol)
- 1 tbsp lemon juice
- 1 tsp lemon zest
- 1/2 tsp vanilla extract
- 1/4 cup almond flour (for the base)
- 1 tbsp melted butter (for the base)

Procedure:

1. In a small bowl, mix the almond flour and melted butter to form a crumbly base. Press the mixture into the bottom of a mini muffin tin.
2. In a separate bowl, beat the cream cheese, sweetener, lemon juice, lemon zest, and vanilla extract until smooth and creamy.
3. Spoon the cream cheese mixture over the almond flour base in each muffin tin.
4. Refrigerate for at least 1 hour until firm.
5. Serve chilled.

Nutritional Values (Per Serving):

- Calories: 100
- Carbohydrates: 3g
- Protein: 2g
- Fat: 9g
- Fiber: 1g
- Sugar: 1g

Cooking Tips:

For extra flavor, top each cheesecake bite with a fresh berry or a dollop of sugar-free whipped cream. You can also add a touch of vanilla bean for a deeper flavor.

Health Benefits:

These bites are low in carbs and high in healthy fats, thanks to the cream cheese and almond flour. The lemon adds a dose of vitamin C, making these bites a refreshing yet indulgent treat.

Berry Parfait with Whipped Cream

This light and refreshing berry parfait is made with layers of mixed berries and sugar-free whipped cream. It's a perfect low-carb dessert that's both simple and delicious.

Time of Preparation: 5 minutes

Cooking Time: None

Serving Units: 4 servings

Ingredients:

- 1 cup fresh mixed berries (strawberries, blueberries, raspberries)
- 1 cup heavy whipping cream
- 1 tbsp sugar-free sweetener (like stevia or monk fruit)
- 1 tsp vanilla extract
- Fresh mint for garnish (optional)

Procedure:

1. In a large bowl, whip the heavy cream, sweetener, and vanilla extract until stiff peaks form.
2. Layer the mixed berries and whipped cream in serving glasses, alternating between the two.
3. Garnish with fresh mint and serve immediately.

Nutritional Values (Per Serving):

- Calories: 180
- Carbohydrates: 10g
- Protein: 2g
- Fat: 15g
- Fiber: 4g
- Sugar: 6g

Cooking Tips:

For added texture, sprinkle some chopped nuts or unsweetened coconut flakes between the layers. You can also add a drizzle of sugar-free chocolate syrup for extra indulgence.

Health Benefits:

Berries are low in sugar and high in antioxidants, fiber, and vitamins, while the whipped cream adds healthy fats. This dessert is light, refreshing, and blood sugar-friendly.

Chapter 11

Diabetic-Friendly Smoothies and Drinks

Green Spinach and Avocado Smoothie

A nutrient-dense smoothie made with spinach, avocado, and a hint of lemon. This green smoothie is rich in fiber, healthy fats, and antioxidants, making it perfect for managing blood sugar.

Time of Preparation: 5 minutes
Cooking Time: None
Serving Units: 2 servings

Ingredients:

- 1 cup fresh spinach
- 1/2 ripe avocado
- 1/2 cucumber, chopped
- 1 cup unsweetened almond milk
- Juice of 1/2 lemon
- 1 tsp chia seeds (optional)
- Ice cubes for blending

Procedure:

1. Add all ingredients to a blender and blend until smooth.
2. Serve immediately, chilled with ice cubes.

Nutritional Values (Per Serving):

- Calories: 140
- Carbohydrates: 8g
- Protein: 3g
- Fat: 10g
- Fiber: 6g
- Sugar: 2g

Cooking Tips:

For extra creaminess, you can add a tablespoon of Greek yogurt. If you prefer a sweeter flavor, add a small handful of green apple slices.

Health Benefits:

Spinach is packed with vitamins A, C, and K, while avocado provides heart-healthy fats. The combination of fiber and healthy fats helps stabilize blood sugar levels.

Strawberry-Banana Protein Shake

A refreshing and filling protein shake made with fresh strawberries, a small banana, and protein powder. This shake is ideal for a post-workout snack or a quick breakfast.

Time of Preparation: 5 minutes
Cooking Time: None
Serving Units: 2 servings

Ingredients:

- 1 cup fresh strawberries
- 1 small banana
- 1 scoop vanilla protein powder (sugar-free)
- 1 cup unsweetened almond milk
- 1 tbsp flaxseeds (optional)
- Ice cubes for blending

Procedure:

1. Combine all ingredients in a blender and blend until smooth.
2. Serve chilled with ice cubes.

Nutritional Values (Per Serving):

- Calories: 180
- Carbohydrates: 22g
- Protein: 15g
- Fat: 5g
- Fiber: 5g
- Sugar: 12g

Cooking Tips:

You can replace the almond milk with unsweetened coconut milk for a different flavor. Adjust the amount of protein powder based on your dietary needs.

Health Benefits:

The protein shake provides a balanced blend of protein, fiber, and natural sugars from fruit, making it a perfect option for keeping energy levels stable without causing blood sugar spikes.

Low-Sugar Lemonade with Mint

A refreshing and tangy lemonade sweetened with a sugar-free sweetener and garnished with fresh mint. This low-sugar drink is perfect for hot days.

Time of Preparation: 5 minutes

Cooking Time: None

Serving Units: 4 servings

Ingredients:

- 1/2 cup fresh lemon juice
- 4 cups cold water
- 1/4 cup sugar-free sweetener (like stevia or monk fruit)
- A handful of fresh mint leaves
- Ice cubes for serving

Procedure:

1. In a pitcher, combine lemon juice, cold water, and sweetener. Stir well until the sweetener dissolves.
2. Add fresh mint leaves and let the lemonade sit for a few minutes to infuse.
3. Serve over ice cubes.

Nutritional Values (Per Serving):

- Calories: 10
- Carbohydrates: 3g
- Protein: 0g
- Fat: 0g
- Fiber: 0g
- Sugar: 1g

Cooking Tips:

For an extra zing, add a few slices of cucumber or a splash of lime juice. You can also muddle the mint leaves before adding them for a stronger flavor.

Health Benefits:

This lemonade is low in calories and sugar, making it a great thirst-quencher for diabetics. Lemons are rich in vitamin C, and mint adds a cooling, digestive boost.

Chia Seed and Almond Milk Smoothie

This creamy smoothie is made with chia seeds and almond milk, offering a blend of fiber, healthy fats, and protein for a satisfying and nutritious drink.

Time of Preparation: 5 minutes

Chill Time: 10 minutes

Serving Units: 2 servings

Ingredients:

- 2 tbsp chia seeds
- 1 cup unsweetened almond milk
- 1/2 tsp vanilla extract
- 1 tsp sugar-free sweetener (optional)
- Fresh berries for garnish

Procedure:

1. Mix chia seeds, almond milk, vanilla extract, and sweetener in a bowl or jar.
2. Let it sit for 10 minutes to allow the chia seeds to expand, stirring occasionally.
3. Blend the mixture until smooth, or serve as is with a garnish of fresh berries.

Nutritional Values (Per Serving):

- Calories: 120
- Carbohydrates: 8g
- Protein: 4g
- Fat: 7g
- Fiber: 7g
- Sugar: 1g

Cooking Tips:

For a thicker consistency, let the chia seeds soak longer, or add more almond milk if you prefer a thinner drink. You can also add a handful of spinach for extra nutrients.

Health Benefits:

Chia seeds are loaded with omega-3 fatty acids, fiber, and antioxidants, supporting heart health and digestion. Almond milk is a low-carb alternative to dairy.

Cucumber and Lime Detox Water

A hydrating and refreshing detox water made with fresh cucumber slices and lime, this drink helps cleanse the body while keeping you hydrated throughout the day.

Time of Preparation: 5 minutes

Cooking Time: None

Serving Units: 4 servings

Ingredients:

- 1 cucumber, thinly sliced
- 1 lime, thinly sliced
- 6 cups cold water
- A few fresh mint leaves (optional)
- Ice cubes for serving

Procedure:

1. In a large pitcher, combine cucumber slices, lime slices, and cold water.
2. Let the water infuse in the refrigerator for 1-2 hours.
3. Serve chilled with ice cubes and fresh mint.

Nutritional Values (Per Serving):

- Calories: 5
- Carbohydrates: 2g
- Protein: 0g
- Fat: 0g
- Fiber: 0g
- Sugar: 1g

Cooking Tips:

For extra flavor, add a few slices of fresh ginger or a splash of lemon juice. You can refill the pitcher with water to reuse the cucumber and lime slices throughout the day.

Health Benefits:

Cucumber is low in calories and high in water content, making this drink hydrating and refreshing. Lime provides vitamin C and antioxidants, supporting detoxification.

Iced Herbal Tea with Fresh Berries

A light and fruity iced herbal tea with no added sugar, this drink is infused with fresh berries and mint for a refreshing, antioxidant-rich beverage.

Time of Preparation: 5 minutes

Steep Time: 5 minutes

Serving Units: 4 servings

Ingredients:

- 4 cups brewed herbal tea (like hibiscus, chamomile, or green tea), cooled
- 1/2 cup fresh mixed berries (blueberries, raspberries, strawberries)
- A handful of fresh mint leaves
- Ice cubes for serving

Procedure:

1. Brew the herbal tea and allow it to cool to room temperature.

2. In a pitcher, add the fresh berries and mint leaves. Pour the cooled tea over the berries and mint.

3. Let the tea infuse in the refrigerator for 1 hour before serving over ice.

Nutritional Values (Per Serving):

- Calories: 20
- Carbohydrates: 5g
- Protein: 0g
- Fat: 0g
- Fiber: 1g
- Sugar: 3g

Cooking Tips:

For added sweetness, you can add a sugar-free sweetener like stevia. You can also experiment with different herbal teas and berries for varying flavors.

Health Benefits:

Herbal teas are rich in antioxidants and anti-inflammatory compounds. The fresh berries add vitamins and fiber, making this a refreshing and health-boosting beverage.

Chapter 12

Meal Plans and Tips for Long-Term Success

7-Day Diabetic Meal Plan

A carefully curated 7-day meal plan designed to help manage blood sugar levels while enjoying nutritious, balanced, and satisfying meals. Each day includes breakfast, lunch, dinner, and snacks, with an emphasis on whole foods, lean proteins, healthy fats, and low-carb options.

Day 1

- **Breakfast**: Scrambled eggs with spinach and mushrooms
- **Lunch**: Grilled chicken Caesar salad (diabetic-friendly)
- **Dinner**: Baked salmon with roasted Brussels sprouts
- **Snack**: Almonds and a small apple

Day 2

- **Breakfast**: Greek yogurt with chia seeds and fresh berries
- **Lunch**: Quinoa-stuffed bell peppers

- **Dinner**: Grilled shrimp with zucchini noodles
- **Snack**: Cottage cheese with cucumber slices

Day 3

- **Breakfast**: Low-carb veggie scramble
- **Lunch**: Turkey and avocado lettuce wraps
- **Dinner**: Pork tenderloin with sautéed spinach
- **Snack**: A handful of walnuts and a small orange

Day 4

- **Breakfast**: Flaxseed pancakes with sugar-free syrup
- **Lunch**: Lentil and spinach soup
- **Dinner**: Grilled Mahi-Mahi with pineapple salsa
- **Snack**: Celery sticks with almond butter

Day 5

- **Breakfast**: Smoothie with almond milk, avocado, and spinach
- **Lunch**: Roasted beet and arugula salad with goat cheese
- **Dinner**: Lemon garlic shrimp stir-fry with broccoli
- **Snack**: Hard-boiled eggs

Day 6

- **Breakfast**: Chia seed pudding with almond milk
- **Lunch**: Grilled chicken with roasted vegetables
- **Dinner**: Baked herb-crusted tilapia with steamed veggies
- **Snack**: Greek yogurt with almonds

Day 7

- **Breakfast**: Low-carb veggie omelet
- **Lunch**: Tuna salad lettuce wraps
- **Dinner**: Eggplant lasagna
- **Snack**: Carrot sticks with hummus

Nutritional Guidelines:

- Focus on lean proteins, fiber-rich vegetables, and healthy fats.
- Limit refined carbs and added sugars.
- Drink plenty of water throughout the day.
- Include a variety of fresh fruits, vegetables, and whole foods.

Health Benefits:

This meal plan helps maintain stable blood sugar levels, provides essential nutrients, and promotes long-term health. The meals are balanced and designed to prevent spikes in blood glucose.

How to Prep Meals in Advance

Meal prepping is an excellent way to stay on track with your diabetes-friendly diet. This section outlines practical steps and tips for preparing meals in advance, saving time and reducing stress throughout the week.

Meal Prepping Steps:

1. **Plan Your Menu**: Choose a variety of meals for the week, including breakfast, lunch, dinner, and snacks.
2. **Create a Shopping List**: Organize ingredients by category (proteins, vegetables, dairy, etc.) to make grocery shopping efficient.
3. **Batch Cook**: Prepare large portions of lean proteins (grilled chicken, turkey meatballs, etc.), roasted vegetables, and whole grains (quinoa, barley) to use throughout the week.
4. **Portion Out Meals**: Divide meals into individual portions using reusable containers for easy grab-and-go options.
5. **Prep Snacks**: Cut up vegetables, portion nuts, and prepare healthy snacks like hummus or Greek yogurt ahead of time.

Pro Tip:

Prepare smoothies in freezer-friendly bags, with all ingredients measured out. In the morning, just blend with almond milk or water for a quick breakfast.

3. Portion Control and Managing Cravings

Mastering portion control is key to managing diabetes and preventing overeating. This section offers simple techniques to help keep portions in check while satisfying your cravings.

Portion Control Tips:

- **Use Smaller Plates**: Trick your mind by eating from smaller plates, which make portions appear larger.
- **Measure Portions**: Use measuring cups and food scales to ensure proper portion sizes for carbs, proteins, and fats.
- **Eat Mindfully**: Slow down and chew thoroughly to enjoy your food and recognize when you're full.
- **Plan Snacks**: Don't skip snacks. Choose healthy options like almonds, apple slices, or Greek yogurt to curb cravings.
- **Avoid Eating from the Bag**: Portion out snacks into small bowls or bags rather than eating straight from the package.

Managing Cravings:

- **Stay Hydrated**: Sometimes thirst is mistaken for hunger. Drink water before reaching for a snack.
- **Opt for Healthy Swaps**: If you crave sweets, try a piece of fruit, or make a sugar-free dessert like chia pudding or almond flour brownies.
- **Practice the 10-Minute Rule**: If you're craving something unhealthy, wait 10 minutes and engage in another activity. Cravings often pass.

Smart Swaps for Your Favorite Foods

This section provides simple and creative food swaps to enjoy your favorite dishes while keeping carbs and sugars low, perfect for a diabetes-friendly lifestyle.

Smart Swaps:

- **Swap Pasta for Zoodles (Zucchini Noodles)**: A low-carb alternative to traditional pasta that pairs well with marinara or pesto.
- **Swap Rice for Cauliflower Rice**: Grated cauliflower makes a great low-carb, fiber-rich substitute for white rice in stir-fries and burritos.

- **Swap Bread for Lettuce Wraps**: Replace bread or tortillas with large lettuce leaves for sandwiches, burgers, and wraps.
- **Swap Mashed Potatoes for Mashed Cauliflower**: Enjoy the creamy texture of mashed potatoes without the high carbs.
- **Swap Chips for Veggie Sticks**: Carrot, cucumber, and celery sticks paired with hummus or guacamole satisfy crunch cravings.

Pro Tip:

Experiment with spiralized vegetables like zucchini, sweet potatoes, and carrots to add variety to your meals while keeping them low-carb.

Best Snacks for Blood Sugar Control

Snacking is important for managing blood sugar levels and preventing overeating at mealtimes. This section offers a list of diabetes-friendly snacks that provide protein, fiber, and healthy fats.

Best Snack Options:

- **Hard-Boiled Eggs**: Rich in protein and low in carbs, perfect for stabilizing blood sugar.
- **Greek Yogurt with Berries**: A combination of probiotics, fiber, and antioxidants.
- **Almonds or Walnuts**: Packed with healthy fats, protein, and fiber for a filling snack.
- **Celery Sticks with Peanut Butter**: A low-carb snack with healthy fats and protein.
- **Cottage Cheese with Cucumber Slices**: Creamy and rich in protein, this snack also hydrates and satisfies.
- **Roasted Chickpeas**: Crunchy and full of fiber, these are perfect for curbing hunger.
- **Veggie Sticks with Hummus**: A fiber-rich snack that provides healthy fats and protein from chickpeas.

Pro Tip:

Keep pre-portioned snacks on hand to avoid overeating and to ensure you have healthy options when hunger strikes.

Building a Diabetic-Friendly Pantry

Stocking your pantry with diabetes-friendly staples is essential for quick and healthy meal preparation. This section outlines key items to have on hand to support your diabetic lifestyle.

Pantry Staples:

- **Whole Grains**: Quinoa, brown rice, barley, and oats
- **Legumes**: Lentils, black beans, chickpeas
- **Nuts and Seeds**: Almonds, walnuts, chia seeds, flaxseeds
- **Healthy Oils**: Olive oil, avocado oil, coconut oil
- **Nut Butters**: Natural peanut butter or almond butter (no added sugar)
- **Canned Fish**: Tuna, salmon, sardines (in water or olive oil)
- **Low-Sodium Broths**: Chicken, vegetable, or beef broths for soups and stews
- **Coconut Milk**: For smoothies, curries, and baking
- **Herbs and Spices**: Cinnamon, turmeric, cumin, basil, oregano, rosemary
- **Sugar-Free Sweeteners**: Stevia, monk fruit, erythritol for baking and drinks

Pro Tip:

Avoid stocking your pantry with high-carb, processed foods that can trigger blood sugar spikes. Keep your kitchen organized with diabetic-friendly foods to make healthy choices easier.

Conclusion

A Healthy Life is a Happy Life

Living with diabetes doesn't mean sacrificing the joy of eating. In fact, adopting a healthier lifestyle can bring more energy, balance, and overall well-being. By making smart food choices, focusing on nutrient-rich ingredients, and learning how to manage portion sizes, you can take control of your health without feeling deprived. Your relationship with food becomes an empowering experience that supports both your physical and emotional health, leading to a happier, healthier life.

How to Keep Enjoying Food While Managing Diabetes

The key to managing diabetes while still enjoying food lies in making mindful adjustments. Opt for whole, unprocessed foods that nourish your body, and find creative ways to reinvent your favorite meals. Whether it's swapping out refined carbs for low-carb alternatives, or incorporating more fresh vegetables and lean proteins, there are endless possibilities to explore.

Focus on balance and moderation, and remember that every meal is an opportunity to fuel your body with the nutrients it needs. By planning ahead, prepping meals, and making smart swaps, you'll find that managing diabetes becomes easier over time, and you'll continue to enjoy the foods you love in a way that promotes long-term health.

Final Thoughts and Encouragement

As you embark on or continue your journey with diabetes management, it's important to remember that progress is more important than perfection. The recipes, meal plans, and tips in this book are designed to help you enjoy delicious, satisfying meals while keeping your blood sugar stable.

Change takes time, and building healthy habits is a process. Celebrate small victories, and don't be too hard on yourself if you face setbacks. The goal is to create a sustainable lifestyle that you can maintain for the long term—one that prioritizes your health, happiness, and love of food.

With the right tools and mindset, you can live well with diabetes, enjoy your meals, and embrace a future filled with energy and vitality. Keep experimenting with new recipes, stay proactive about your health, and always remember: a healthy life is a happy life!

Made in United States
North Haven, CT
16 November 2024

60425456R00050